1

The Core of Humanology and How to Configure Other Human Minds

By Ron and Victoria Bloom

The Core of Humanology and How to Configure Other Human Minds

By Ron and Victoria Bloom

Bloom and Cloud Solutions LLC

Yeadon, PA USA

Published by Bloom and Cloud Solutions LLC

Yeadon, PA, USA

Printed in the USA

Library of Congress Cataloging – in – Publication Data

Bloom, Ron and Bloom, Victoria.

The core of humanology and how to configure other human minds

ISBN 978-0-9983014-6-4

1. Self help
2. Psychology

CONTENTS

Introduction:

Welcome back, my friends, to the philosophy of configuring the mind. We must note that this book requires a prerequisite, which is reading *The Core of Humanology and How to Configure the Human Mind* (2016). This is essential in order for one to understand the principles and procedures in this book. The reason being is that these principles and processes don't change. The same philosophy stressed in *The Core of Humanology and How to Configure the Human Mind* is the same strategy you will deploy when trying to configure other human minds. You can't even begin to fathom how to achieve this ability if you yourself haven't mastered the techniques on you! *The Core of Humanology and How to Configure the Human Mind* was based on configuring your own mind for growth and objectivity. This book is going to focus on how to configure the everyday human minds you will encounter in your life. Whereas *The Core of Humanology and How to Configure the Human Mind* was for your own personal enrichment, this book is to aid you in configuring the mind of others in order to get them on your program! Interaction with other humans is critical to your success, and it's extremely important that you know how to deal with all types of folks. With that said, let's start configuring other's mindsets that propel you to your goals!

Chapter 1: Core

If you passed the course of *The Core of Humanology and How to Configure the Human Mind*, you should have a solid core already in place. You should already have a solid foundation from which your core values stand upon. It's time now to deploy those same strategies outlined previously to figuring out the core of others. Again, I'll repeat my disclaimer: if you haven't read *The Core of Humanology and How to Configure the Human Mind,* close this book. It will be like reading braille if you haven't learned how to use the alphabet. The principles I will speak on in this book are the same in the previous book. The only difference is rather than downloading them into your system for understanding you, you are uploading them into other's system for understanding you! This is critical when dealing with other humans.

I want you to ask yourself, "How swell your life would be if everybody understood your views and complied with all your desires?" Think about that for second! You would have the perfect life with no restrictions or conflicts. We all know that this will never ever be the case. Hence, wars, politics, religions, divorce, infidelity, and many other aspects give credence to this hypothesis. However, even with that said, you still can give yourself a better chance to obtain your goals if you can configure other's mindsets. For instance, convincing your boss to give you a raise helps you obtain financial goals you might have. Another example is convincing someone to have sex with you. (LMAO) We all know what that satisfies! How about convincing a car salesman to cut down on the price of a car you desire? This helps you obtain the goal of purchasing some wheels.

You see, we have to configure other's minds every second, every minute, every hour, every day, every week, every month, and every year of our lives (24/7 factor). The only way to achieve configuring someone else's mind is to get at their core. Just as the core is a set of values and foundations for you, it is to others as well, if they have one at all. Those who don't have a core will obviously be a little more lenient in gaining access to their mind for configuration. However, you must possess the ability to gain access to even the most difficult anti-virus systems!

Whereas before you were developing your own anti-virus system, now you must learn to infect other systems and upload your programming to achieve conformity to your goals. This is an intricate process and more than often requires tedious work in order to be successful. To be honest, depending on the strength of the other's core and foundation, you might not ever achieve it. Whatever the case, the theory is if you can engage someone at their core, you give yourself a good chance at getting them to conform to your goals. Moreover, you are still steadfast in your approach of standing firm on your own core values and foundation. This will only build upon your growth which can possibly lead to a future solution to infect somebody's strong anti-virus.

So how do we get at someone's core? You need only to start with yourself. This is where the prerequisite *The Core of Humanology and How to Configure the Human Mind* kicks in. You first must state what makes you tick, right! What makes you you, such as happy, sad, likes, dislikes, ideology, religion, etc.? This is what you must find out about the individual you are trying to configure to your program. You must first find out what makes them tick.

Wise man once said, "Different strokes for different folks." Therefore, your objectivity should always be the first vehicle you deploy when trying to penetrate someone's core. The ability to learn a behavior or ideals foreign to your own is important for penetration (objectivity). You must have the willingness to portray what another individual holds dear to their core and make it believable.

For our purpose, let's define this as politics. Isn't this notion at the core of every politician? This is why politics is deemed a sweet science. It is a systematic approach of configuring many minds with conflicting views that all see one individual as believable. This happens because the politician was able to penetrate their core and infect their foundation with the (emotion) of trust. The politician usually succeeds in their goal of gaining votes to obtain a government position. However, the victims of politics usually don't see the rewards of their vote unless it is near and dear to the politician's core!

The number one reason for this is usually voters who are disappointed with an official they helped elect didn't do their homework on the politician. They broke one of the cardinal rules from *The Core of Humanology and How to Configure the Human Mind,* that you never take someone's word at face value. Moreover, they often fail to educate themselves about the politician through the scientific method and draw conclusions from the politician's previous actions.

This can be such actions as previous words spoken, voting record on political measures, and enacting their own policies.

With that said, from this point on I want you to start deploying politics to every individual that you interact with in order to configure their mind to obtaining your goals! When you are trying to crack someone's core, you can't come at them full throttle with your ideology. There are several reasons why this isn't a good approach. For one, you can deter an individual from even opening up to you on an interpersonal level. Interpersonal skills are crucial to infecting another individual's core with your ideology. As the word implies, interpersonal means to get inside someone (inter) and learn their principles (personal) that govern their lives. Depending on the individual's (foundation) you are trying to infect, you should also be able to gauge how firm they stand on these principles. If your core values are detrimental to the person who you are trying to infiltrate, you will more than likely be denied access. This again is also gauged by the person's (foundation).

This is absolutely not the path you want to take when dealing with other humans. Due to the impact of our social necessity, it is crucial for one to be able to get along with another person! I don't need to speak on folks who you have to interact with on a daily basis that can make your life miserable. You see part of cracking the code of someone's core through politics and interpersonal skills is to just be able to coexist peacefully! You are not always going to be able to completely make someone conform to your ideology. It's virtually impossible. However, if you can create a peaceful coexistence, then you still have reached your goal of a stress-free environment.

Remember, humans tend to rely heavily on their comfort zone and will dispel any notions of exiting that utopia (regression). Your job as an invading virus onto an unknown entity is to first gain the trust of your host! In order to do that, you must first at the very least gain some preliminary information about the host you are trying to invade before unleashing your subjective onslaught of ideology. Don't get me wrong, there are going to be many people you encounter who at first glance seem to share the same core as you do. I said at first glance because as we know from *The Core of Humanology and How to Configure the Human Mind* consistency in action, word, and fact are what will ultimately determine the person's true core.

Keep in mind for all you know, the other human you are trying to configure might be deploying the same scientific approach of politics as you are. Wise man once said, "When someone says or shows you who they are from initial contact, you should believe them." This quote holds value only when self-portrayal from initial contact is validated through words, actions, and facts. However, as we just explained the essence of politics, that doesn't necessarily mean that's what the person is actually about (core). It can be a defense mechanism from a flawed core and foundation, it can be the truth, or it can be politics deployed to crack your core! You see, what you must understand here is that configuring another human's mind is tedious and sensitive at the same time. You are going to have to deploy interpersonal skills and politics to gain access to one's core. This is all bundled in your (objectivity)

11

from *The Core of Humanology and How to Configure the Human Mind.* Then, you have to remain consistent in your approach all while refraining from deploying ideology from your core that is in conflict with the host you are trying to infect.

The goal is to see eye to eye with the other human on common grounds. Then hopefully their defense mechanisms will begin to give way and you can begin to understand their true nature (core). With a better understanding of what makes the person tick (core and foundation), then you can begin to methodically try to configure their minds to your aspirations. Remember as I always eluded, everything is intertwined together here. The politics, interpersonal skills, being methodical and consistent are crucial to cracking someone's core. The ramifications are simple. You are either going to obtain all your goals with assistance from other humans in which you configured their minds to do so, you are not going to achieve some of your goals because of failed relationships of humans you couldn't configure, or worst of all, you aren't going to achieve any of your goals because you can't configure anybody's mind to your aspirations.

One mishap when trying to configure someone's mind could lead to a failed relationship! This will ultimately impact your bottom line of achieving a goal! For example, what happens to a politician when they are entangled in a scandal? Usually in some capacity, they tend to lose some if not the majority of their supporters. This happens because the scandal is usually indicative of what the politician said they are not about (core and foundation). The question of their integrity, trustworthiness, and ethics usually comes into play.

The supporters they stand to lose are their colleagues on Capitol Hill and even more importantly, people who voted them into office. The obvious ramification here is the inability to pass legislation and ultimately losing their job.

This is the same way in which a mishap playing politics with another human can lead to your doom. You have to consistently meet the other human's expectations on common ground before you can ask them to pledge their allegiance to your agenda. Jumping the gun too soon can be catastrophic to your cause! For example, if the politician wanted to engage in an activity that's detrimental to their supporter's core, they should at the very least wait until after they get out of office. Promises unfulfilled generally can cause a politician to lose his or her support network. This is why you are going to have to back your words up with action in order to maintain the support of your potential host.

You see, what the sweet science of politics tells us is that we must suppress our urge to display our natural tendencies. Politicians carry out their true intentions through back door deals that rarely hit public awareness. This is how they can maintain a support base and still carry out their true intentions. If all politicians were to make their true intentions known while campaigning for office, they would stand to lose some supporters. This obviously is not conducive to gaining a political title. A politician needs all the support they can get and this is no different from you!

This is another reason why you don't upon initial contact with someone spill the beans on you! You want to remain a chameleon in order to get to the stage of configuring someone's mind. You want to be able to sway their support once you are past their core's defense. The objective is that your interpersonal skills break down the defense mechanisms to their core, and your political skills break down their (foundation) for configuration. You must remain steadfast with this approach throughout the entire relationship with your host. You will be surprised at how many people set themselves up for failure from divulging too much information to another individual way too soon. The repercussions don't always come from the onset of initial contact. Sometimes, the information you give away will come back and bite you in the ass much later in life.

For instance, let's say you just met someone and you confided in them about your personal life. Let's say you told them about your habits of infidelity! Let's say you and this other individual had a friendship for a couple of years, and then the relationship soured for whatever reason. Now usually when a relationship sours nowadays, one or both parties involved in the separation become vindictive towards the other. I think you can guess what I'm going to say next. The information you provided them on your infidelity can now come back and haunt you if the other person plans on deploying it as an attack mechanism! They can tell your spouse and disrupt if not end your relationship! This is when you see on social media outlets people getting caught cheating or exposed! I bet you nine out of 10 times their undoing was in part of the mouth running like a broken faucet!

Wise man once said, "Wise men listen while fools run their mouth." The information you provide is never safe in the mind of another human. Objectivity dictates that one you don't know all who this human knows, you don't ever truly know their motives, you don't know who else is configuring their mind, and for what purposes. This is why configuring someone's mind is so difficult because you have to show and prove your talk all while masking your true identity. At the same time, you must remain aggressive in your approach of extracting as much information you can out of your host to help you gain their support. Remember, it may be that you can't configure this person in a lifetime, but hopefully your interpersonal skills can at least keep the host on common ground with you.

The idea here is not to allow any other human to become a deterrent to your goal; therefore, if the battle to configure the other human's mind becomes a draw, that's still a win for you. This is the essence of the wise man quote, "If you can't beat them, join them." This is on the common ground level and not on a level that is detrimental to your core and foundation, of course. At the same time, as I say, "If you can't beat them join them," you are still redeveloping your plan constantly to garner their support 24/7. Remember the principles from *The Core of Humanology and How to Configure the Human Mind* are still in effect here. The script doesn't change. EVER!

As you can see, the chapters are outlined in the same way as in *The Core of Humanology and How to Configure the Human Mind*. They are just applied differently instead of self to another person. So, as I mentioned about interpersonal skills, they are crucial in breaking down someone's defense mechanisms. As I also noted, they are bundled in your (objectivity). You see, getting to know someone weighs equally heavy on the foundation just as it does on their core. Understand this!

You can learn a foreign language easily and be able to communicate with another person in their native tongue effectively. This gives you grounds in breaking their core's defense, but just knowing their native tongue is useless if you don't know about their culture (foundation). This is how politicians lose support with certain groups consistently because they speak the language of the group (core) but they fail to understand the culture of the group (foundation). They fail to display validity when it comes to understanding the culture of the host they are trying to configure.

For example, my interpersonal skills may be inclusive of speaking the language of the host I'm trying to infect with my ideology. You might be able to communicate with the host along the lines of their preference but that still doesn't make you one of them! Understand this! You have to dig deep well beyond communication and indulge in the host's culture in order to have any chance of configuration. Remember, you have to be validated to knowing the crucial aspects of the culture. When you speak the language and know the culture, this gives you far more leverage in configuring the host's mind.

For instance, a politician who speaks about constructing policies beneficial to a certain group of people is speaking the language (core) of that sector of hosts. However, if that same politician isn't validating that claim by displaying with action proven knowledge of the culture, then that politician will be deemed suspicious. This in return will obviously affect the amount of support he or she will get from the host population. On the other hand, if that same politician speaks the language and indulges in the culture of the host he or she is trying to configure, they will more than likely be deemed by the host as one of us!

For example, a politician that's running for office on a platform of minority empowerment and is a minority will most certainly have better leverage than another politician who is not of the targeted host. They can both have similar platforms for minority improvement but the minority candidate will seem more valid from the fact that he or she is one of us! So, in essence, speaking the language is only going to get you so far, but when you couple the language aspect with knowing traditions, values, diet, music, fashion, etc., your host will be more inclined to open up and allow you to configure their mind! Then and only then you can begin to play politics.

You have to be able to possess the ability to get someone off their foundation in order to configure them. Keep in mind the philosophy from the previous book as it pertains to core values and the foundations from which they stand. Understanding what makes a person tick (core) is only half the battle. The war comes when you try the shake up the foundation from which the core values lie upon. Let's dwell on how politics can help you break down your host's foundation and aid you in configuring their mind to your aspirations.

Chapter 2: Foundation

Politics is the sweet science that will allow you to break down someone's anti-trust mechanisms. The best way to get people to engage in your aspirations is to gain their trust. We say use politics because the sheer fact of the matter is you are not going to like everybody's core values that you have to engage with. However, you are going to need these people as well in order to achieve your goals, be it under the 24/7 factor. The individuals who share the same principles as you are really not applicable for the use of politics. Obvious reason is they will pretty much follow in line with much, if not all, you stand for. They are the easy ones to help you reach your goals.

However, as we mentioned before in *The Core of Humanology and How to Configure the Human Mind*, you must mostly prepare for unforeseen circumstances. In the case of configuring other human's minds, you need to have a plan for those individuals who take a different stand from your core values. Politics! You see political parties don't worry too much of pleasing their constituents in their own party as it pertains to issuing policies because they have already configured each other's mind to a partnership (others who are aligned with most if not all of the same core values). They only need now the majority cooperation of the other political parties to fall in line with their aspirations. They generally will have solid disagreements on policies, but at the end of the day, each side is going to have to configure enough minds from the other party in order to pass legislation.

If this cooperation doesn't happen, usually it results in unachieved goals from one political party or all involved. This is because if the cooperation isn't there from the parties involved, then the usual repercussion is black balling each other because one side didn't get their way! You see when configuring other's minds, you can't afford to be black balled by anyone! Just as you have seen before with the U.S. government, when black balling is in full affect, nobody wins and the entire system shuts down.

This is the ugly side of politics that you don't want to enter in when dealing with other individuals. You must tread in steep water and carefully play politics with other's minds. At the same time, you must remain steadfast on your core values and foundation. The reason why government doesn't cooperate is due to mostly outside interests that influence their minds! These include business enterprises, other politicians, voters, international relationships, family, and much more. You don't have these influences with dealing with other humans in the government realm. Some may apply, especially business dealings, but essentially you are trying to configure the everyday citizen on a micro scale.

So, as you engage in politics to get someone to trust you, your best tool to deploy is kindness. Wise man once said, "Kill 'em with kindness." This is the doorway from which you can try to enter. There are some things in which almost every human can be influenced by, and kindness ranks way up there! The main reason why people don't kill each other with kindness is due to that nasty emotion of like and its derivative perception! You see, people are extremely judgmental and are quick to cast individuals out of their life who have different core values as they do. Even though you think you might be doing yourself a favor, in the long run you could be doing yourself harm.

For instance, how many times have you seen a politician's past relationships come back and bite them in the ass? For example, when a politician talked down on another politician and now the latter politician is in a position that is someway persuasive over the position that the former politician currently has. This rift is undoubtedly going to cause some friction for the politician who in the past has talked down on the leading politician.

Another example could be if you don't associate with a coworker for whatever reason and that person ends up becoming your supervisor. This could possibly affect your job status in many different ways! These things happen every day! The other employee you shunned off could have a disdain for you now and might start heckling you with their newfound power! This is why your teacher always told you in school that the nerd you are picking on now will someday be your boss. This is the principle behind that theory. You see when people disassociate with people on the basis of perception or differences in core values that are minutely detrimental to your own, they tend to let their emotions carry out assaults on that human's character. Rather than "killing 'em with kindness," they display disdain in several ways. You see, people notice when other people don't like them through their actions and words. At least they should! This is because you let emotions govern your actions in which is an absolute violation of a sound, configured mind! Those emotions are going to convey disdain to the other human for most of all interactions or non-interactions you have to engage in with that person.

For example, how many times have you heard a politician under fire due to the fact of a conversation they had with someone else in regards to another politician? This is the non-interaction aspect that can come back and bite you in the ass! The straight up interaction aspect obviously could have a more imminent impact but it still doesn't help your cause either way. Your goal is to have everyone and their mommy in line with your aspirations! Some of the ways you can show disdain of people are actions like not speaking to them, avoiding them, talking down about them to others, direct aggression from yourself, body language, and even physical aggression. Direct verbal and physical aggression are an obvious sign that someone has disdain for another! That's obvious! The hope is that the aggression wasn't due to perception but due to imminent jeopardy of your core, health, or life!

The important thing to remember here is that politics weighs heavy on the small things first, then the macro. Wise man once said, "A smile goes a long way!" You will be surprised how many people develop a synopsis of your character based on first impressions and small actions. When you greet someone with a smile, it is usually received a lot better than a greeting of a neutral posture or worst a frown! Even if the first impression wasn't your best foot forward into somebody else's foundation, you can still reverse the perception with consistent kindness killing! You obviously don't want to get off on the wrong foot and play catch up because it is not always the case you can reconfigure someone's mind once it's made up.

Remember, you just don't want to coexist with someone peacefully; you want them in your pocket as a tool you can use for personal enrichment! This is why a subtle thing like a smile can literally go a long way. Marriages, business partnerships, business deals, getting a job on interviews, getting extras at a restaurant, friendships, etc., have all started generally with a warm greeting that was accompanied by a smile! Think about that concept for a long period of time because if you don't get the essence of that wise man statement, you will ultimately fail at configuring other human's minds.

Think about how a politician always court potential voters with a smile. They are trying to break down the potential voter's anti-trust system in order to gain a vote, or they are trying to reaffirm their position in the voter's foundation for them to vote for him or her again. That simple subtle gesture can make a huge difference in the fight to gain support of your goals. Subtle things like saying hello on a consistent basis, engaging in friendly conversations, including the individuals on your thoughts of them (positive only), offering help to individuals, express concern for individuals, investing in individuals, socializing with individuals, and much more are ways to win influence over others.

You see, when you deploy such subtle actions as the ones mentioned above, you can place a strong footing in one's foundation as someone they can trust and align themselves with. This is the essences of a friendship! You want someone to be able to call you a friend, no matter how deep down inside you feel about them on a personal level. You have to keep it implanted in your mind that no matter how that person treats others, when they are in your presence they are aligned with your aspirations, so long as their actions aren't detrimental to your core!

Remember, we are speaking of configuring individuals' minds that has minor disruptions to your core or none at all. Obviously, if someone is detrimental to your core you avoid them altogether if possible or just coexist with them peacefully. At the same time, you still deploy the act of "killing 'em with kindness" in an effort that they may come around in the future, but you absolutely walk a fine line with it not to go asshole backwards! Remember, peaceful coexistence is a win because it is the mass appeal at the end of the day that will carry you to your goals. If you have 26 out of 50 people aligned with your ideology, you have given yourself a chance to achieve your goals. At the same time, you are hoping that the peaceful coexistence of those 24 not aligned could foster an alignment in the future. That's why you must engage those individuals on an interpersonal level. You need to understand, or at the very least, have a persuasive demeanor that you understand their positions and are willing to align yourself with their ideology in some form of compromise.

Wise man once said, "We must agree to disagree." This quote is the definition of a compromise. Both parties involved will not get everything they want, but both foundations will remain mostly intact. Moreover, in the end, nobody gets fucked! This is why before you engage in politics you need to have a strong core and foundation as we mentioned previously in this book. You have to understand that a person who doesn't have strong core values and foundations can be easily persuaded to trust you, which can aid you! At the same time, they can be easily persuaded to hate you, which can be detrimental to you too!

The best way you can prevent such is having a strong footing in their foundation, and that takes consistent effort. This is why I mentioned such tactics like investing in individuals. Understand this when we speak on interpersonal skills, we speak on the principle of making someone feel your words and actions through their soul! With that said, you must learn to go above and beyond to get at one's soul. By the way, soul is just the sum of one's core values and the foundations for which they stand! Consider soul as an abbreviation for core and foundation for your reading purposes. Understand that just asking someone who you see physically or mental shaken how are you doing, getting their response, wishing them well in the future, and then going about your way is a half assed job when trying to get to someone's soul! You need not only to engage that person with expression of concern as we just did with the first scenario by asking how are they doing and wishing them well, but you need to couple that with offering help and investing in that individual as well.

Wise man once said, "A little bit of kindness goes a long way." You need to help that person anyway you can so long as you are not going asshole backwards and it's not detrimental to your core. For example, giving a person a ride who's struggling to walk goes a longer way than waiting patiently at the light that you granted for them to pass. This is an example of investing in an individual by using your time and vehicle and at the same time offering help. This person will remember you far longer than just letting them pass at the light you had the right of way to. The political move you made could help develop a relationship that in the long run could be beneficial to you.

Wise man once said, "You never know who you might need in this lifetime." This is why you have to be political at a moment's notice under the 24/7 factor because you never know where your fortunes may lie. For instance, I remember when once I passed a stranger on the road that was trying to flag me down for some assistance with his car. I initially passed him but I had a change of heart and turned around to go assist him. I remember thinking at the time how many times my car had broken down and how I felt hopeless in those situations. I chose to invest my resources and offered help to this individual on the political notion that hopefully if I'm ever in that situation, somebody would reciprocate the same favor for me. When I engaged the guy he stated, "I ran out of gas trying to get to the gas station," and if I could give him a ride to a gas station so he can get some gas and come back to his car. By the way he greeted me with a smile upon my arrival like a dog happy to see its master! No lie he was happy as shit! (LMAO!) I obliged to his wishes and engaged him with conversations of my ordeals with my car. After it was all said and done, he offered me money for my time and efforts, and I declined. I told him that I was just happy to lend a hand and was satisfied with that. He thanked me and we exchanged numbers to stay in touch with each other. I honestly didn't have any intentions of staying in touch with the guy because my perception of him was that he was young and immature which at the time, I wasn't engaging individuals like that at all.

Keep in mind this is one of the moments in my life in which helped me develop the principles I'm speaking of now. I was on my way of configuring my mind but was not quite there yet! At this point in my life I was still driven by emotions, not facts! So as the story goes on, true to my unsound mind at the time, I didn't call or return any calls from the guy. It just so happens I was going to my barber for a routine line up, and this new barber I never seen before was in the shop. He says to me, "Hey man, what's up how you been?" I'm looking like huh! Do I know you? He says, "You don't remember you helped me when I ran out of gas a while ago." Some time had passed and I forgot the dude's face, but I then begin to recollect. I was shocked that he even remembered me, and doing what I did touched his soul. Especially the part of me doing it pro bono. I say that because he gave me free haircuts for the duration of the time I remained in the area. The reciprocity only stopped because I moved to another state. Now get this, we never actually ever socialized outside of the barber shop but what kept him consistent in his approach was the fact that I helped him out in a desperate situation and asked for nothing in return. He felt compelled in his soul to somehow repay me and free haircuts was that! True story! That obviously helped me out with a core of saving money!

Who would have ever known that simple act of kindness would have paid for itself ten times over! Keep in mind the move was political in nature because I was only doing it in efforts to get reciprocal efforts from someone to

26

aid me in my goals! Go figure! This can happen for you to but you have to remember the founding principles of *The Core of Humanology and How to Configure the Human Mind.* You have to put yourself in position in order to gain these alignments to your goals. These are the same principles, just different aspects of application. You have to patronize as many people's minds as you can in order to give yourself greater chances of success in this lifetime. Those who pose differences in ideals shouldn't be casted away from your life just because of an emotional perception of them being disruptive to your core. You see, I saw the guy as being disruptive to my core. Therefore, I never actually socialized with him outside of a haircut, but my political and interpersonal skills allowed me to still save money! You see over time he realized that we had different core values and he respected my choice not to socialize yet still saw me as a friend and gave me free haircuts! The political aspect here is I still got his vote even though I felt differently about him socially! He still saw me as a person he could allow to patronize his foundation. I know this because of interpersonal conversations we had about each other's lives.

This is how you must position yourself with other humans on a micro scale. I say micro because each person is their own character and comes with unique anti-trust systems you have to conquer. This is what will bring us to our next step in configuring other's minds, and that is reflections. Same format folks, just applied to a different scenario. Politicians can be up one minute and down the next. This is due in a large part of how difficult it is to sway the masses all while trying to keep individuals happy. This is why politicians set up polls on how they are doing with certain demographics throughout their tenures. It is extremely important that they keep majority of each demographic in order to keep their job or at the very least majority of the most popular. However, remember we want the most people we can have in our corner in order to push our policies, right! Think about it like this, even if you have the vast majority of one demographic that can get you elected, you still have opposition out there that can sway people in the majority that elected you! This can eventually turn into a negative for you if enough of your majority can be swayed to oppositional thinking. That's why you need most people aligned with you as you can in order to suppress opposition. This is why it is very important to see how well you are received by the people you are trying to configure. Just as you reflect in the mirror to see how you have progressed with the relationship with yourself, it is now time to reflect on how well your relationship has progressed with another person. Let's dwell on reflection.

Chapter 3: Reflection

As we have mentioned, the probability of success is through precise measurement of the current plan implemented to reach a goal. You can't proceed with a flawed plan that isn't going to allow you to achieve a goal. You must stop, evaluate the current situation, confirm or deny the plan you implemented is working, reconfigure your focus if necessary, and continue to push forward with your agenda. The same principles of reflection of your life apply to reflecting on your position in other's core and foundation. As you are reflecting on how others are receiving your input, you must carefully measure how well you are penetrating their soul.

One mistake of perception of how you are positioned in one's soul can ultimately lead to disruption or destruction of a goal you are trying to obtain. This is why it is extremely dire that you judge your position in someone's soul correctly because it can unravel all your efforts of configuration in an instant. For example, how many times have you gone on a date, thought everything was going well, and the date ended up a disaster? Perhaps your date asked for sex, and you weren't ready to go their yet! How did that affect your psyche? Did you think of the date differently? Did you feel as though this was the individual's only motivation? Did your suspicions rise to a level of distrust in your potential suitor? Did this ultimately change your mind of courting this individual? This is what happens when you misjudge the host in which you are trying to infect with your ideology.

Just as we mentioned earlier, generally when these situations arise on a date it is due to pushing your agenda on one's soul too rapidly and misjudging. Wise man once said, "Trust is earned, not given." It is irrational to think another person is going to fully entrust you to their soul when initially meeting them. Don't get me wrong either, some people don't have a strong foundation and therefore it is possible to reach their souls rather quickly! (Sex on the first date. LMAO!!) Generally speaking, however, it will always be a wise decision to play your cards methodically until factual evidence gives you a highly probable reason to believe you have successfully penetrated someone's soul. You see, people who have rocky core values and shaky foundations are easy to penetrate. Hell, you don't even have to work for their minds at all; they just give it to you! You have to keep in mind that the vast majority of people aren't that easy, and even if they were, each individual still will have to be engaged differently due to natural characteristics. Also note you will never honestly know what's going on in somebody's head. The best thing you can do is reflect on their interactions with you and through the scientific method, draw a conclusion on where you stand with them.

This is why you must move judiciously because if you sense a glimmer of rejection of your ideology, you can quickly redirect your plan in order to not totally lose your host. If you move too fast, you can miss this area of recouping and instead have your plans demolished. For example, if your goal is to sleep with your date on the first night, it is not professional to just tell your host what you want especially when at the very least, they haven't given you a glimmer into their soul. You see a professional soul hacker first tests the waters! You have to learn how to get answers in a roundabout way without actually saying what you want or mean! So instead of saying can I have sex with you tonight, gear up an innocent conversation around the matter that doesn't incriminate you as desiring that. Then gauge the responses through words, body language, and actions to start formulating a consensus of the person's character.

For instance, say you and your date have a mutual admiration for an entertainer and that entertainer was caught naked on camera. This is highly plausible nowadays, right. Cameras are everywhere! You say, "Hey did you see them get caught ass naked in that viral video?" If your date responds something like, "Yeah how gross, and they should have been careful," that should give you a red flag that this person's character may be on the lines of a conservative and rushing into intimacy might not be a priority. On the other hand, if the response is something like, "Hey if you got it flaunt it, and I'll do the same thing," then this should give you a glimpse of hope that their character might be more liberal, and if you play your cards methodically, you may have a shot at romantic bliss! It can go either way though. A person could be liberal on the subject of nudity and also be conservative on the subject of sexual relations. Again, play it slowly, and don't let emotions get involved in your quest of conquering someone's soul.

You should already know about emotions from our first book! So, while reflecting on how someone is accepting your input, there are some key elements that are crucial for you to gauge success. Nothing new here folks; it's the same ole scientific method. Only difference here is instead of stating your own problem first, you are stating your desired wants from another individual first. You see, when you are trying to configure someone else's mind you shouldn't put emphasis on correcting their personal problems. Rather you should place emphasis on how you want them to treat you! You need to place importance on what you want them to do for you. Keep in mind (objectivity) always rules supreme, and it may take you to slightly help them get their mind right through strategic planning. But it should still be in the realm of your ultimate goal of receiving what you want from them in order for you to reach your goals.

For example, a person who is using someone for money and the person who they are using has an addiction that is sucking up profits, so to speak, you might want to engage in a plan to reconfigure that person's personal addiction problem in the grand scheme of being able to retain more of that person's money. It just makes sense! That will allow the person using the addict to persevere much better if the addict has more money to take. The rationale of not worrying about the host's personal problem is simply due to the fact you don't want to lose hindsight of your objective. You don't want to get sucked into that person's cause. Worrying about them ultimately plays to their hand because it disrupts your desires and you have to make sure you're not overly compensating one individual in the chess match of configuring multiple minds at once. This could blow your cover!

As we mentioned earlier, politicians often fail when they compensate only one segment of the voting population. In order to maximize success, you need the cooperation of the masses, and compensating one individual could be seen as deal breaker with other people if you have already planted in their soul that you are aligned with their causes, which might differ with the individual you are overly compensating! This is crucial! It is not worth losing five supporters over one person!

Also playing devil's advocate, wise man once said, "One man's trash is another man's treasure!" You have to understand that somebody's personal issue could be in turn a positive for you! If taking advantage of somebody's issues helps you achieve your goals, take advantage so long as it is not detrimental to your core, and the negative repercussions for doing so are minimal. Keep in mind that the Supreme Being whomever you worship gave you a mind. It will never be you fault if they don't use it to prosper in this life! This is why your mind has to be configured right first before you engage in configuring others.

Now we said you must conjure up what you will need from this particular person or people in order for you to achieve your aspirations, right. This goes back to our first book with proper planning. For instance, if you want to become a successful manager, what does it take to achieve that? You make the tree, right? Then you develop strategies and plans from this tree. So, on our tree should be at a minimal knowing the scope of your industry, obtaining a job in the industry, getting staff to perform productively, getting along with your supervisor, getting along with other managers, etc.

Now let's say under the subtree of knowing the scope of your industry is education. In order to get your education, you will most likely have to attend some form of educational institution such as college or a trade school. Now think, who are the type of people you are going to want to configure their minds to your aspirations? The instructor of course is an obvious one. Why? You want the instructor to give you the knowledge you need in the industry, a good grade, and mentoring beyond class. You see you might say as a rookie of configuring other's mind that the professor is already obligated to teach the students the materials they need in order to maintain employment. This is true but it is often a minimal requirement. You want to go far beyond just the syllabus. You want to engage the instructor on an interpersonal level. You want to reach his or her soul. Why? Think about what else other than a good grade and knowledge of the industry the instructor could possibly provide you. How about connections to a possible job in the future, a good reference, ongoing support through your career, information not available in your textbook that could help you in achieving your goal, ideology on other life aspects that could help you grow, etc.?

You see these are just some of the things that you can garner from reaching someone's soul in this particular instance. It is still all in the grand scheme of you achieving success. The only thing you have to do is couple your desire of what you want out of the instructor with going above and beyond the average student. You see the idea here is the more you get someone to like you, it is harder for them to do anything that will disappoint you! For example, I deployed this strategy on practically all of my former instructors and I remember one in particular that stood out as a good example of what I'm speaking on. I had a math instructor in which at first, I didn't see eye to eye with. I was young and still developing my mind and hadn't yet mustard an understanding of the consequences of my actions. Long story short, my actions landed me in the hot seat during one of my instructor's class lectures. I was verbally reprimanded for my behavior during my instructor's lecture and I immediately changed my behavior. I was threatened with being expelled from class.

I later reconciled with the instructor through the methods of which I'm speaking on now and actually formed a solid relationship with the professor that lasts to this day! This relationship paid off for me in a major way when it came to the end of the course. I was doing quite well in the class and on the final exam I needed a score of at least a 90 in order to secure a 4.0 grade for the course. I remember going up to the professor with my test in hand after I finished the exam and I felt confident that I had aced it. Prior to the professor grading the exam we shook hands, and I gave him one final cordial embrace for all he had taught me during the semester. He graded the text and I ended up actually scoring an 85 on the test. I remember this well; it was like clockwork as he and I almost simultaneously threw our hands up in shock that I missed my average by a measly 5 points. He then collected his pen and to my surprise changed my score to a 90 in his grade book and told me congratulations on a good job! This was obviously a person whom I had touched their soul to go against the regulatory rules of his employment to look out for me! This obviously aided me with my core of graduating and embarking on a career in my respective field.

Now under the scientific method, I had to state the problem. The problem was I needed a good grade initially, and I had to fix the unforeseen problem of being under scrutiny of possibly being expelled from class. The hypothesis is simple: if I don't get my shit together, I could possibly fail this class, get expelled from this class, possibly followed by getting expelled from school altogether, risk not getting accepted by another institution, risk not meeting my goal of graduation, risk not developing a career, etc. These scenarios were all detrimental to my core. Thus, incorporated in my hypothesis was hopefully mending the relationship with my professor to alleviate these possible foreseen issues.

Then comes the next step in the scientific method and that's the experiment. As I mentioned before, when you are trying to enter one's soul you have to make that shit believable and stay committed to the cause! I first started out my experiment of mending the relationship with my professor by simply apologizing. You see, as I mentioned previously, a little bit of kindness goes a long way. Moreover, admitting guilt is a solid offensive move when you have wronged someone! Remember that!

Wise man once said, "The truth shall set you free!" I coupled my apology with acting according to his guidelines in class and staying after the sessions shooting the breeze to get to know him better. During these talks I came to acknowledge how much he loved coffee and when American Education Week came by, I surprised him with a gift card to his favorite coffee shop. Remember, "Kill 'em with kindness!" At the same time, I was analyzing how well he was receiving my advances on his soul! He reciprocated his acceptance of trust in me through little things like telling about his personal life, giving me heads up on pop quizzes, giving me information on my career path, etc. I was at this point comfortable in saying that I was making legitimate headway into his soul, if I wasn't there already but I still played it easy!

The conclusion of this experiment was simply that through factual evidence, I more than likely succeeded in configuring the professor's mind to my aspiration. He changed my grade for me which could have been detrimental to his core of maintaining employment if his superiors found out.

That's what you must have the ability to do for you. You must maintain the ability to keep people in your corner for the duration of your life, not just for the moment! You see this is what differentiates someone who is a user of another human and one who knows how to configure someone's mind for their gain. There is a striking contrast when the two techniques are deployed. You might be reading this book and thinking, "I have to get good at using people to my advantage," and that ideology will ultimately cause you to fail at configuring another human's mind.

Understand that when someone typically is using another human, it is just for a temporary gain and once the goal is achieved, they cast them aside. Moreover, their true colors tend to show after they have used and abused their host. The relationship usually ends and the two entities may never mingle again. For example, when someone is in a relationship with a partner who is just using them for money, and the user leaves the host because they go broke. That's a classic user, right! You see they are no longer committed to the relationship because the well has run dry! Their goal was financial support and stability. The notion that somebody doesn't have the means to support them is detrimental to the user's core. They are gone to try to infect another host with those means. They can care less about the broke host they were infecting because the only thing they see is self-preservation! That's what classic scrubs, gold diggers, manipulators, and yes players do!

That is in contrast to what this book is teaching you. This book is on the premise that you never know who you might need in this lifetime. Moreover, you will need the cooperation of others to get to where you want to go in life! With that said through the lens of objectivity, you should keep your options of relationships at a bare minimum of cordial encounters. Meaning, even if you were able to configure someone to reach an objective, you still keep the relationship moving in a positive manner. You don't have to have a deep involvement, but the relationship should always be accessible.

Wise man once said, "Keep your friends close and your enemies even closer." I like this quote because the narrative is prompting you to remain optimistic in your view of others. You see, the user who left the host because they were broke in the previous example did so because they are selfish. Generally speaking, selfish people tend to have a subjective point of view 99% of the time. Therefore, if you are not down with their cause it's fuck you and now you are the enemy.

On the other hand, the objective configuring person sees a host who doesn't conform to their ideology as still having potential with aiding them in the future. Who's to say that the broke host doesn't become richer by chance! You just don't say fuck 'em because you can't have your way with their mind! You keep working at it until you find that common ground. At the same time, you are ultimately keeping the door open for opportunities for yourself that might arise when you don't cast someone aside such as being able to now benefit from their newfound wealth.

For example, how many people do you know whose spouse broke off the relationship with them, and then came running back when they thought the grass was greener on the other side? How many ex-bosses have you used for a reference? How many you couldn't use for references? What nerd in school is a billionaire now that you turned down their advances in school? What coworker did you bicker with and now they are your superior? These are some of the questions you have to foreshadow before you cast someone away as an enemy.

You see that wise man quote I just mentioned about keeping your enemies closer means much more than just the traditional meaning of enemy. When people think of enemy they tend to think of the traditional meaning of a physical foe, war adversary, opponent, etc. That quote is more so speaking on the mental capacity of enemy. You see as mentioned earlier, if you have a subjective mind then you will cast out anything or anyone that doesn't comply with your school of thought. This ultimately causes one to shut down doors before they open and refrain from dealing with certain individuals. They see people who don't conform as the enemy mentally! They don't want to be anywhere near their enemies because it's against their core and foundation. They will truly stand to lose out on growth due to this mental subjective approach on life.

On the other hand, like how the first book taught us, it is wise to live your life through objectivity. The lens of objectivity will not display the potential host an enemy you cast aside but as an enemy you can learn from. Thus, you keep them close just as well as you do the people who conform to your ideology! I want you to remember this because it is a crucial element when configuring other's mind. Wise man once said, "It take a dummy to know one." This quote is stating that if you want to learn how to do something, you have to learn from someone with experience.

With that said, it will take your enemy to tell you the ideology that is in contrast with yours in order for you to understand why, possibly develop an antidote for it, if not on that person, perhaps another one with the same ideology! This is why you keep your friends close and your enemies closer. It goes back to how to configure the human mind in which you always strive to learn and grow mentally to conquer life's challenges. In this case it's configuring other human's minds. Same principles, just different areas of applications! This is why you must stay committed to conforming someone to your ideology as much as possible! Let's explore how we stay committed to the cause of self-preservation through the lens of objectivity!

Chapter 4: Commitment

The ability to stay committed to configuring someone's mind is the key to success for a lifetime of configuration. As we mentioned in the previous chapter, the trick to configuring someone's mind is just not about obtaining a goal. It is about earning their unwavering support throughout your lifetime and theirs. Wise man once said, "It is ok, they will need me again." This quote is not the limelight you want to be in when configuring another human's mind! This quote entails the negative effect of being used and vowing never to be used again. Remember this book is not based on the ideology of use and dump. Rather, it is continuing to use the person forever within the compounds of good graces! Once you put this quote in somebody's mind, you can call it opportunity lost. It will be most unlikely you can ever consort with them again for anything. This is detrimental for growth because you never know who you might need again as the quote implies!

This is why you have to remain committed to peacefully coexist with others at the very least. The ultimate goal is conformity, of course. Remember if you agree to disagree, that is still a start in the right direction. The key here is you aren't casting anyone out as an enemy. Rather you are keeping that enemy close for a learning opportunity. The longer the door can stay open, the better chance of conformity. If the door closes, slim chance at configuration! That is plain and simple! This is what staying committed to configuring other's mind helps you do and that's refraining from the pitfalls of closed doors to opportunity.

You see, as before when you committed to do something for yourself, you were prompted to give yourself a timetable in order to gauge your effectiveness and achievements. When you are configuring the minds of others, there is no timetable. You go non-stop under the 24/7 factor and never let up until your death! You see, you can properly gauge yourself and how well you are doing with your own commitment on something, but it is difficult to say how long it's going to take to configure someone else's mind. In fact, your goal is to configure their mind until death anyways. That's why setting a timetable is null and void in this particular area.

You want to continuously update the host's mind to all of your new ideology and have them continue to aid you in obtaining goals. This is why your commitment has to be 100%, 24/7, because it is absolutely necessary with the ongoing battle of the minds! You see, just because you and another see eye to eye currently, who is to say that it won't change overnight? Remember, we mentioned earlier that you are not the only person out there configuring minds! Your host could be getting input from another source that may garner more attention than yours. This could ultimately sway the host's mind and priorities as they pertain to you. This is why you have to constantly cement your ideology and will onto your host to maintain their cooperation. This is how you can see a couple married for 30 years and suddenly divorce! This is why you have to remain committed to configuration of your host because there is always a new virus on the horizon that is poised to override your outdated input!

Now we discussed some of the tools we use to gain entry to someone's soul, such as "kill 'em with kindness," etc. Here is where you multiply and refresh those tools over and over again. What do we mean when we say multiply and refresh? First of all, it's commitment, right. Thus, you have to constantly display through action and word the definition of the phrase "kill 'em with kindness." What we mean by refresh is constantly evolving your actions and words to keep pace with possible invasion from others on your host.

In summary, you don't want to become stagnant in your approach to configuring someone's mind. You should reasonably assume that just as you have goals and your mind changes like the wind, the host in which you are trying to infect has the same qualities. Therefore, you have to maintain the ability to adapt to the changes in your host and still remain committed to selling them your dream while at the same time, adhering to their dreams as well.

You see, ultimately this is how configuration of another's mind fails when one becomes stagnant in their approach to doing the job. The job never stops. Therefore, you should always educate yourself on how to do it better and become more efficient at it. This is how a relationship of 30 years can dissolve in an instant. One or both parties involve stop supporting the other's ideology (configuration lost).

For example, let's say a person meets someone and successfully engages their attention (interpersonal skills) enough to obtain a date with them. Obviously, the goal is to hopefully have a good date and engage in a relationship eventually. Let's say it all goes like clockwork, and the couple is fucking like rabbits (conquered the host's soul) for the first year of their courtship. Now let's say the sex has fizzled a bit and one individual still desire the fireworks that were obtained during the first year. This is where configuration has the potential of breakdown on the host still desiring rabbit sex because it can be perceived as a lack of interest from the other partner in the relationship.

We all know what lack of interest can do to a person's mind if it isn't configured personally right? Are they cheating? Is it me? Is it my body? The perceived lack of commitment in your host's mind could lead them susceptible to advances of another party because of your perceived lack of commitment to the relationship. This happens quite often than not! This is how a long-term relationship can end abruptly and seemingly without any cause.

Think about how many shows you see on TV dealing with couples experiencing infidelity in their relationships. What are some of the clichés the cheating partner uses? You never show me any affection anymore! You're never there when I need you! You don't treat me like you used too! You changed and I don't know you anymore! This is when commitment is perceived to be lost in the eyes of your host, and your configuration gives way to another invading host. This obviously affects your goal of maintaining a relationship.

You see, if your goal is to maintain a relationship you've successfully configured somebody's mind to, you have to in some capacity maintain the elements that got it rolling from the onset. Then over time multiply those elements and refresh them to meet the current mindset of your partner in the future. This is committing to the goal of retaining this relationship.

On the other hand, think about how many times you watch those same TV shows and what does the victim of the infidelity usually say? Why did you do it? Haven't I done everything? Why after all this time? Why him or her over me? What did I do to you to deserve this? They generally seem clueless on why their spouse is cheating on them, right! It's like everything just totally came out of left field. This is because they became stagnant in their approach on the relationship. They didn't remain committed to being in tune with their partner. Their partner no longer believed that they were in line with their core as they were with her or his (configuration lost). This is why you must reflect constantly in order to see if there are signs your configuration is still working.

Remember, we mentioned earlier that strong interpersonal skills are inclusive of the ability to listen and learn how one thinks or feels in order to reach their soul. This is why your commitment to configuring another's mind weighs heavily on your ability to listen, learn, adapt, and communicate with your host (reflection). You can't remain committed to something you don't know how to commit to properly! Your goal of a healthy relationship with the individual is appropriate, but how can you expect to maintain it if you aren't in tune with that person's desires? Remember everything is intertwined. We mentioned that you have to be vigilant in reciprocating your support of your host's goals as well, right. Therefore, you must listen, learn, adapt, and communicate with your host on an interpersonal level (reflection), and through (core) and (foundation), action coupled with words, reciprocate your support of their desires ongoing (commit).

This is why we mentioned earlier that you don't want to come at someone with your ideology full throttle from the onset. One reason, you don't want to deter them from your configuration, and two because you don't want to let all your tricks out the bag too early either as it pertains to commitment. Remember, ongoing mind configuration is a slow methodical process and some humans can essentially become tired of your shit so to speak! This is why you have to methodically deploy tactics as they are running concurrently with the present state of mind your host is in. It will be fatal to your longevity of configuring your host's mind if you deploy the wrong tactic too soon or too late!

Wise man once said, "Leave something to the imagination." You have to keep you host interested in the idea of following and supporting you. This is why you see a lot of celebrities always trying to up the ante in their endeavors to maintain appeal. If they got half naked in a video or post, the next time they are fully nude. Now in case you notice, those celebrities eventually fade to obscurity as the next best thing comes along unless their artistic performance is just that superior. On the other hand, a more conservative artist that doesn't go that route will more likely maintain appeal for longer than the more liberal artist.

Why you think that might be? For one, the artist, if they gain some noteworthy appeal, has to have a decent performance in their sector to gain fans. With that said if they are conservative, they will let their art speak for themselves, not their body. Now let's say the artist's music isn't as popular as it once was and the artist decides to reinvent themselves specifically the way they portray themselves in public. Let's say they start displaying seductive photos of themselves and advertise them as such. This has the potential to awaken old fans who were intrigued by this notion of seeing the artist in such a seductive way and new fans who possibly like what they see; at the same time, they can be open to listen to what the artist performs.

This is a prime example of how not letting all your tricks out of the bag too quickly can help you in the long run. I think anyone with a configured mind would say it's better to start out high, get low, and recapture glory in the twilight of a career rather than starting out strong and fizzling out in your prime never to recapture glory. So, in the long run, which scenario has more longevity? You must maintain a methodical approach when trying to configure someone's mind! The goal here is to never give up on configuring another individual's mind. You have to develop a thick skin when it comes down to rejection. You are going to need the ability to let rejection of your advances on someone's mind flow off you like water on a duck's back! You can't get frustrated and even worse let your frustrations become apparent to the host whom you're trying to invade!

This is critical on two frontiers. First of all, you have allowed your emotions to cloud your judgment and impede progress towards your goal. This is in direct violation of configuring your own mind and as I have mentioned several times thus far, if your mind isn't configured, then you can't configure another person's mind, let alone the fact that you'll be able to get configured by someone else! Second, you never risk the chance to gain an ally, as long as it's not extremely detrimental to your core. You have to get off your high horse (pride) and let rejection roll off you like a bead of sweat. Then, you have to keep plowing and try to get that individual to go along with your goals or obtain a peaceful coexistence.

Let's dwell on this particular principle for a moment, shall we (pride). This is what causes a lot of relationships to either end or become fragile. Majority of people in this world just can't come down off their high horse (pride). This is because of those antagonist emotions and opinions combined. We spoke of the ills of these thought processes in the first book, and they start to become more critical here in this aspect of your life if not yet treated. Hopefully, you have and this is just a reminder of why it is so important to configure your mind correctly before venturing into the treacherous waters of configuring someone else's mind! Keep that in mind, no pun intended (LOL).

Understand this, when you get pissed at someone when they reject your advances of a romantic relationship, you've already lost the battle of configuration. When you get angry when you hear someone making unsavory comments about you, you've again already lost the battle of configuration. Understand this, rejection can never be the end all when trying to configure someone's mind. It should only be received as a minor setback, and as we have learned from the first book, you should have learned from that rejection and in development of the next plan to conquer your host's mind. After all, that's what configuration is all about. You are trying to program a system that will operate in the exact fashion you desire. Until the process is perfected, there are going to be some bumps in the road (rejection), but there is still a chance to configure someone's mind, for mistakes learned will pave the way towards a goal!

Keep in mind that every war that has been won came with some lost battles! Wise man once said, "You may have won the battle but you haven't won the war." I want you to think for a minute how many couples are together who were once sworn enemies, how many archrivals in high school are now best friends as adults, how many products that came out in the consumer market that were failures at first and now thrive, how many musicians tell the story of how their music was rejected by some and now they are at the pinnacle of success! This is because the person or people spearheading the configuration of others to get them aligned to their goals refused to succumb to rejection. They pushed forward (commitment) and didn't let a battle lost deter them from winning the war of their goal.

Your mindset has to be I'm going to make you love me, no ifs, ands, or buts about it! Your mind is going to be aligned with my goals one way or another! So, let's get back to the example that you hear someone say something unsavory about you. Notice I said hear as in with your own ears, not heard it through the grapevine. Remember, we brain fuckers only base our configuration of others and thyself on facts only! So, you know for a fact at the very least for whatever reason this person you're trying to configure sees you in a negative light.

Now a person who hasn't configured their own mind yet may see this as a need to protect themselves from this individual, retaliate in some form, or just not patronize this person's mind at all. The battle of configuration is already lost with this mindset, but if you read *The Core of Humanology and How to Configure the Human Mind*, your approach is the scientific method and getting to the bottom of a problem with a systematic approach. You see just because you heard the person speak ill of you, that doesn't actually mean they despise you! They actually might just be a weak-minded individual who's been configured to think ill of you by another person who actually despises you! Ever thought about it like that?

That same person who speaks ill of you may actually become useful in the future to ward off attempts of character assassination from the original person who configured them to think as so. This is of course after you let the initial rejection run off you like water on a duck's back and reconfigure the hell out of their mind! Remember, when you are configuring someone's mind, you are not only configuring them but you are also configuring all the minds that they patronize as well. You are planting the seeds that will help you succeed in life through interactions with other humans.

For example, once you have configured your boss' mind that you are a hard worker that could lead to a better job through him or her by way of promotion at your current job, a new job at a different company your boss might have obtained and brought you along, or via reference from your boss to one of his or her peers at another job that can use your skills. Have you ever thought about it like that? There are literally millions of scenarios we can discuss why a strong commitment to configuring other's minds is important, but they will all fall under one umbrella and that's achieving goals. Now that you hopefully get the justification of why you need to remain committed to configuring other's minds, let's dwell on the systematic approach you use when configuring unique individual's minds (plan implementation).

Chapter 5: Plan Implementation

Wise man once said, "Some things are worth fighting for." This includes your ability to prosper in life, of course. You see, there are three things that stop a lot of people from configuring or trying to configure other's minds: laziness, anxiety, and fatigue. Many folks have the aspirations of configuring people's mind to their goals, but sometimes they get complacent when things aren't going as they had planned. They then fall in those categories just mentioned above: laziness, anxiety, or fatigue. That wise man quote personifies the commitment of staying the course until satisfaction is met. There is no room for complacency when trying to configure another human's mind or maintaining the configuration thereof.

As I mentioned before, you must remain diligent when configuring other people to your cause because it only takes one time for you to take your foot off the gas pedal and lose your host! Now you should recall from the first book, in order to see your dreams to fruition, you must have a sound plan. This is the same as configuring the minds of others. You must develop a solid plan that will enable you to invade your host and let your virus configure them to your program as best as you can.

Again, as with any plan, you have to develop it off facts, not emotions, opinions, or propaganda. Since we are talking about another person, the obvious thing we need to do first is get to know your target. You need to know what makes that person tick just as you evaluated your own self from the first book. You need to know their desires, dislikes, likes, favorite food, color, etc. You need to gather as much information as you can before trying to configure someone.

Remember, we said configuration is a methodical process, and one wrong move can cost you an important ally to your goals. Thus, gathering as much information as you can before invasion is critical when formulating a plan to conquer a host's mind. You see, as we mentioned earlier, this information is going to be compiled with your interpersonal skills that will hopefully get you in the front door of the person's mind! The more you know about the person, the more scenarios you can use to break down their defenses. This helps you develop your plan because you will then know the do's and the don'ts of what will keep your host satisfied with you.

Once you have gathered enough information and determined if this person could be of importance to you reaching a goal, it's time to formulate your plan. Keep in mind, interpersonal skills are only part of a plan to configure somebody's mind. The other part, the actual plan, is what sets your goals in motion. For instance, it is a big difference from using interpersonal skills to gain friends to using interpersonal skills coupled with a plan to get a friend to buy you a car! Stark difference! The plan to configure for a goal of yours goes well beyond just a normal interaction with others. The person must now go from associate to becoming an extension of you whether in your presence or absence.

It takes a lot for someone to take on your responsibilities and dismiss their own so tread carefully as you try to configure another's mind. One misstep can cause a serious emotional reaction from someone that can cause you serious harm. So please again, be damn sure that the person who you are trying to configure is worth it to you.

So, once you have established a person's value to you, it's time to reel them in. The first part of your plan should be to determine what you actually need from this person in a specific time frame. This should all sound familiar from configuring your own mind, right! You need to know how much and how long you need this person's abilities to aid you to meet your goals. Remember the factors who, what, when, why, and how when establishing a plan. (When) is definitely a critical part of planning an invasion of somebody's mind because it can make or break altogether! We already discussed (who) as you have established a candidate to help you reach your goals. The (what) is the thing you want to obtain from the host that aid you in your endeavors. The (why) is self-explained, the importance this thing weighs on your success in which the host possesses. The (how) is what methods you are going to take in order to extract the thing you need from the host in order to obtain your goal.

For example, let's use a romantic relationship from a male's perspective to explain how to plan configuration of another's mind. Usually our examples are unisex but since we are showing how to configure somebody else's mind, we need to focus on one person only. Ladies you can always flip this scenario and make it your own (LOL). So, let's say I'm a single guy, possibly starving for a home cooked meal, horny because obviously single, ummmm not getting any ass (LOL), and I'm in need of just good ole' fashioned companionship. For one, my needs are already apparent, of course, along with all the rest of my core values right! This is the (what) I'm looking for when I try to configure my new boo's mind! Now the only thing missing is the (who) I'm going to try and configure to obtain this goal.

Let's say I explore a popular dating site in order to obtain a host. There I meet a potential host in which I deem initially could be the girl I'm looking for. This is when I start gathering as much information as I can from this individual trying to develop a plan of entry into the host's mind. This is if the host accepts me of course but even with rejection, you still plow forward with a new host.

Remember the wise man quote that started this chapter off, a relationship is essential to one's own mental health. Therefore, you fight to obtain this goal for your overall health. So now that we have gathered what we deemed enough information to try and get into the host's head, we need to establish the (when) we are going to try it! This can be as simple as contact from email correspondence to phone conversations, phone conversations to live face to face phone chats, or phone chats to dates. Of course, you are using your interpersonal skills coupled with the knowledge you have already gained from the host themselves to break down initial defenses. You have at this point been using the (when) factor step by step methodically moving towards your ultimate goal of obtaining companionship. You systematically broke the ice of evolving from email correspondence to phone conversations, phone conversations to face to face chats, and face phone chats to an actual date. Again, it took interpersonal skills in order for the girl to gain trust in you from each stage but also a plan of (when) you were going to take it to the next step.

Keep in mind that this is just still for the most part interpersonal skills at work here. The girl is opening up (allowing access to the mind) but she isn't in love with you yet (configuration)! That's when we get to the (how) factor. (How) am I going to get her to the ultimate level of sharing intimacy with me and all the other core values I mentioned I wanted? Dating is one way as you continue to woo your potential host. Perhaps partaking in her interests is another, showing her the value you can bring to the table, etc. Now if the fairytale comes together, you should be able to cure your blue balls by making love to your new host! Remember though that was only a part of your desire. You yearned for companionship and overall mental stability in the area of a relationship. Therefore, the game is not over yet. In fact, it's just the beginning.

You see, we touched on it in the beginning without saying it, but we just reiterated its importance, and that's the (why) factor. The guy wants a solid relationship in order to fulfill his goals along with having someone by his side aligned with his core values. Now if the fairytale continues, hopefully the girl will accept a marriage proposal and a true love connection will be established. Then once married, this is when you should be able to start the configuration process of her mind. It should be reasonable to assume that if a person is willing to take a lawful oath of connection with someone, they are willing to conform and comply with your wishes in order to sustain a marriage.

You ever hear people say it's totally different when you're married compared to just being boyfriend and girlfriend? Whether you know it or not, configuration has a lot to do with it. You see each party is now trying to secure their partner that much more so you may hear demands thrown around like you can't wear that anymore, wear your ring everywhere you go, you can't hang out late anymore, you can't go to the club anymore, etc. These demands usually are bipartisan because the goal of each party involved is to keep the spouse until death does them apart! Of course, the demands can vary widely due to a couple's core values but be assured like death and taxes, new demands will come! This is also a part of the (how) factor in maintaining your marriage just as it was getting to the configuration thereof.

There is a high percentage of marriages nowadays that dissolve, so I don't think it's a secret that it's easier to get married than stay married. You see, regardless of the situation, it all goes back towards your plan to configure another human's mind. The (why) factor is just as critical here too! Remember we said that you have to ensure your purpose of configuring somebody's mind as worth it for you or it can turn out to be detrimental to your core.

For example, how many people you see regret getting married from the financial burden they took from divorce, the strained relationships with children, custody battles, property battles, etc.? You see, I used this example of marriage to showcase the stamina it takes to maintain mind configuration, in this case a lifetime, and to spotlight that when you configure a mind that went wrong, the serious repercussions you can sew. Now as I always say, everything is intertwined

57

in this book, and for a good plan to work, everything has to be in collusion for the same purpose.

As we learned from the first book, a flawed plan will most certainly derail your goals. This is no different than a plan to configure somebody's mind. The plan has to be for a legitimate purpose on all the values you seek, not just a percentage of them. You have to be able to obtain all the goals in which you seek, or the plan you deploy will not be cohesive to a legitimate purpose. The plan could face self-destruction upon detonation because you forced it to try and work, but the contradiction from which you have now created will most certainly cause your plan to go haywire. This is in part because the values you set from your core aren't being fulfilled and they will most certainly antagonize you coming from the same person whom you tried to configure half assed!

Two huge points here! First off, you should never stray from your core values unless it's a new measure that improves upon your previous position in life. Second, you will be configuring somebody's mind that isn't totally on board with your values in which negative repercussions can come from that. For example, let's go back to marriage. A marriage is supposed to be a written doctrine of love and dedication to another individual for a lifetime, right! This should be the only reason why two parties join hands in holy matrimony. This only and nothing else!

Now it is a cold hard fact that there are a large percentage of marriages that fail. Why is that? Think about it! Look at society today. We already said that a marriage is based upon the doctrine of dedication and love with guidelines to help couples reach that goal, right! Now honestly, what do you see driving marriages nowadays? I see finances, prestige, fame, sex, religion, emotions, etc. driving people to tie the knot. The current vows set for marriage are merely a byproduct of what is driving some folk in today's society. However, the vows are the (why) and (how) you are supposed to get married and the byproduct is supposed to be eternal love and relationship. When you are trying to configure somebody's mind you have to keep clear vision of (why) you are doing so and it has to have a significant importance on (how) you achieve your goals.

For example, a lot of marriages end due to infidelity. This can arrive from a multitude of things but the rationale here is one, if sex is that strong of a value for you, then you need to leave your partner in a civil manner and go forth to pursue your goal. (Why) stay with them and pursue actions that can come back and be detrimental to you in the long run? You see, a person who takes the position to stay vaguely committed to their spouse is configuring that person's mind that they are steadfast on their vows they made to them; at the same time, they are also configuring another individual's mind that they love them as well. This is where the turmoil starts! A person who usually cheats on their spouse yet remains in the relationship is usually doing so for reasons other than fulfillment. It can be financial, it can be religiously based, it can be kids, it can be because of fame, etc.

Wise man once said, "People want their cake and eat it too!" You see, the premise of this book teaches you to have your cake and eat it but allow others to partake in eating it with you! You can never be totally self-absorbent if you ever want to configure somebody's mind! It doesn't work!

Reciprocation is extremely important when trying to configure somebody's mind as we alluded to earlier in this book because it most certainly helps in repelling negative repercussions from configurations gone wrong as well!

With that said, then what happens when cheating spouses get caught being unfaithful? This is when you hear things like, "I'm sorry, I didn't mean it, I love you, please stay with me, I'll change, you caused me to cheat, you were never there, etc." Now there are several repercussions that can come from this infidelity. For one, the other values in which you treasured can be lost to divorce. Your family can be divided. You can have a financial pitfall, and nowadays it is even severe as losing your life! Again, (why) does this happen! This happens because a cheating spouse configured somebody's mind to marriage in which all of the cheating spouse's core values were not met! The fact of the matter is you tend to know how compatible you are sexually to someone within the first few times of sleeping with them! If that's the case, why marry them on the value of other principles fulfilled knowing you still have a yearning for a good fuck! It just doesn't pan out! You should not come off your core for any reason at all unless for self-improvement.

Remember, we said configuration is a slow and methodical process, right! With that said, what is the rush? You have to get all the facts about your host before pursuing configuration again as we alluded to already. This is another reason why marriages fail, because people don't get to know each other fully before jumping the broom! Then later on they want a divorce because the person changed. No, the person didn't change; you just didn't methodically get all your ducks in a row before you said I do. The right configuration for dating someone who you are not feeling sexually intrigued by is to first, through an objective lens, give the person a (honest) description on how you feel (facts) and then set forth a reasonable timetable (when) in which you are willing to see if improvement is noted!

Remember our principles from the first book! First, honesty comes from your own (self-reflection) that you truly feel you are not the issue during sexual activity. Second, the facts have to be without emotional influence, as with everything we do, but with cold hard facts like we as partners should be able to climax, and reciprocate pleasures that each of us can enjoy. The notion here is that if the sex is the only thing that conflicts with your core values and all the other boxes are checked off, then it may be worth it to give your partner a chance to conform before you cease the relationship. The key term here: cease the relationship!

Two positive outcomes can come from this methodical approach. One, the partner can actually improve and you can go on and have a great marriage in which otherwise might not had happened if you jumped the gun! Second, you can withstand the pitfall of a failed marriage by dissolving a relationship that was detrimental to your core but possibly retaining some of the good qualities in the individual whom you were trying to configure as a romantic interest to now a friend! This is why you share your cake with others! This is why you never stay so self-absorbent that you lose hindsight of the big picture, which is maintaining the integrity of your core and pursuing your happiness to the fullest.

That's what configuring your mind and the mind of others all is about! It is not intended to fill the glass halfway and become a settler of dreams unfulfilled. Rather its intentions are to carry you to fulfillment and beyond all limitations! This is the reason (why) you remain with radar precision, steadfast on (why) you are configuring somebody's mind! This is (why) you approach (how) you are configuring somebody's mind to be in collusion with your goals methodically. This is (why) after you are done analyzing the host (who) you are trying to infect with your program (what), you figure out (when) you are going to invade.

Thus far, we have established the easier roles of engagement. The (who), the what, the why, the how! For example, let's take the marriage again. The (who) is a spouse of particular origin, gender, etc. (another human). I'll even add a dog or horse in there as well for those into bestiality! This book is objective so whatever floats your boat (LOL). The (what) is the substance in which you are trying to obtain from the (who) that's going to aid you in reaching goals. The (why) is the critical importance this individual can play in aiding you to reach your goals in conjunction with setting up time parameters. The (how) is procedures and methodical processes that are going to be deployed in efforts to configure the host's mind. That brings us to the (why) now, right!

I know we dwelled on this a little already in this chapter but coupled with (how) it begs to have a little more emphasis in balance with the other principles. The (who) and (what) are always subject to change but more importantly they are subject to change with bare minimal negative repercussions to deal with! Understand this, you can always change a target (who) because if you are following the guidelines of configuration of others you should have already rationalized through an objective lens, fact only, and emotionless state of mind this person's worth to your life's goals. Obviously if the person is worth it, then you move forward because the risk of configuration outweighs the rewards, but if you deem the person unsuitable to your needs, you can easily dismiss them before entering into a realm of configuration with no harm done! This is the same for the (what) and (why) because you can always change platforms to your core as you see fit for improvement. Thus, you can always change your perspective of (why) or (what) you need from a person as your goals change or evolve. Again, this is all premeditated (before) you deploy (when) and (how) you are going to configure someone!

Again, if the protocols are followed, there should be no harm to you if you never act on your desire to configure. You see this contrasts with the action of actual deployment. A thought is in your own head only to be scrutinized by yourself during reflection and is shielded from outside ridicule. On the other hand, your actions are visible and once made public, they become subjected to mass scrutiny from others! For example, how many times have you confided in someone and that knowledge from which you divulged became shared with others in which you didn't intend for them to hear! You see that action was at the mercy of scrutiny once deployed for the public to hear. From there it can be ammunition for your enemies to try and harm you. It can hurt your cause greatly. It can ruin your reputation. It can get you fired. It can end your friendships, and much more. It can literally go either for or against you, but rest assured once your true motive is put in the public spectrum, you are subject to scrutiny!

Now if it's a planned effort and the scrutiny is worth it whether pro or con then so be it. However, if it is not part of the (plan implementation) the unforeseen circumstances that weren't accounted for can prove very disruptive to your goals. You can lose configuration not only to the host but to other potential people as well. There's no return once you try to configure somebody's mind! Your credibility and reputation will be on the line and you will have to put in serious work to maintain it going forward, during, and after mind configuration.

Again, tread your course wisely! So (when) do we go for the gusto? This is a very tricky matter that requires a strong grasp of the prerequisite interpersonal skills. You have to be able to break somebody down to their core in order to have any type of access to their mind. Even with the mastery of interpersonal skills, it is the rule of thumb to look at everything through an objective lens. Meaning in this case of trying to configure somebody's mind, you have to understand that it is impossible to depict exactly what at any time someone is thinking. This is why you try to figure somebody out with the scientific method as best as you can. The only difference here is that your tests quite possibly won't yield results right away because in order to get accuracy of what another person's core is, it has to be exhibited through actions coupled with words! You should remember that from the first book, right!

As with everything, it is extremely foolish to go off face value when trying to configure somebody. A person's actions are ultimately what are going to give you the best indicator of when to deploy your configuration. Keep in mind it's not bullet proof. Other people are busy trying to configure you as well. Thus, monitor your host's actions thoroughly before, during, and after configuration (reflection).

Remember always, actions speak louder than words! With that said, base your model of engagement on when an individual goes out their way to either harm you or help you. Remember, an individual who's trying to harm you still needs to be configured as well! We stated earlier that a peaceful coexistence is just as valuable as totally configuring somebody to your goals as well. Regardless of pro or con, both configurations will take the exact same effort. You see, when a person goes out their way whether is for your best interest or not, this is (when) you need to strike.

Let's talk about the pro side of this equation for the moment. A wise man once said, "Fight fire with fire!" I couldn't agree with this quote anymore for the simple fact it's more times than not that a situation will require you to take the exact appropriate action that either your protagonist or antagonist is deploying. For example, when you get sued, usually each party obtains a lawyer to do battle in court. When you're in a fight, usually each party is trying to strike the other, or when you are in a relationship, usually each party "should" deploy loving tactics equal in weight to each other, etc. As you should recall earlier, we mentioned deploying the tactic of "killing 'em with kindness" as it is part of your interpersonal skills set along with reciprocation thereof, right!

This is when it applies to engaging someone through action and word, displaying your kindness in the model of possibly being aligned with your well-being (goals)! This is when you strike because at this point, when a person goes out of their way for you, the symbolic meaning could be a willingness to be configured by you pursuant to your goals! At this point, you should, when engaging with the possible host, be well beyond just cordial interactions. Rather you should now be engaging the host on a more intimate level!

For example, let's say you are just meeting someone and over the course of a period of time you remain cordial with them throughout the timeframe (interpersonal skills). Then let's say one day during another cordial experience the small talk happens to be about coffee and your inability to obtain some. Then let's say the day after that upon cordial interaction with the possible host you are surprised by that potential ally with a cup of fresh Joe just like you like it! This is when it is time to strike and reciprocate that type of action (fighting fire with fire) coupled with (deploying mind configuration)! You see, this is when the person has gone out of their way because you honestly didn't request this from the individual. Rather, it seems they did it from the kindness of their heart. Accordingly, the heart is said to be where the soul lies and if that is the case, this is why you are deploying mind configuring tactics for the simple fact that configuration takes entry to this very level of a person's anatomy! Simply put, this is the only way you can configure another human being period!

It is far easier when a person is allowing this entry to their core as opposed to breaking down their defense mechanisms. This is why you must strike immediately while that window of opportunity is open with strong interpersonal skills and a strong implementation of a plan that's going to optimize configuration and maintain it from that point on (how)! This is why we just stated that once the threshold of cordial interaction has been supplanted by soulful interaction, there's no room for regression back to cordial interaction.

Wise man once said, "No sense in going from sugar to shit!" This is true as it pertains to trying to configure somebody's mind! Your hopes of trying to configure somebody's mind will be derailed by the host's own reconditioning of their mind about you if you go from sugar to shit! For example, on a cordial basis, "Hi, how are you?" with a response of "Fine, and you?" is ok if the interaction with the possible host is still on the level of trying to gain entry to the soul. However, once you have gained entry to the soul, those cordial interactions should now be replaced with such conversations, such as "What did you do last night? How are the kids? How's hubby or wife? What are your plans for the evening? Do you want to hang out? Let's do lunch together, etc." You see now, the conversations should be more than just passing by cordial greeting. They should now be literally good lengthy conversations as you display interest in the potential host's well-being.

The moment you go back to just hi and bye changes the narrative of your potential host's mindset about you! They are going to wonder why all of a sudden you aren't patronizing their mind as you once were. This could ultimately prompt them to reconsider your status in their life which will impact your ability to configure their mind. You see, they may start thinking that the relationship wasn't what they were expecting it to be or become! They will most surely detach themselves from the situation as status of friend, associate, wife, husband, and worst of all, potential host! You see, you can't put somebody on cloud nine and then all of a sudden, they are back on the ground running with you.

Wise man once said, "What you did to get that person is what you need to keep doing to keep that person!" This is the purest definition of "going from sugar to shit." You are ultimately going to lose what you should be striving so hard to obtain. That is the configuration of another's minds to your core values and goal. For example, we said earlier most marriages end in divorce in large part due to infidelity. I bet you if you were to poll divorced couples, a large percentage of them will say they ended the marriage because their spouse changed by way of habits, how they treated them, their attitudes, their sexual desire, work habits, etc. There will be many excuses why but the common denominator for all will be they changed from who they used to be prior to the marriage. Accordingly, who they used to be prior to the marriage is what attracted their spouse to them in the first place. Thus, once these changes happen, it is how a marriage can go from sugar to shit quickly!

Same thing with friendships, if you don't continue engaging your friends as you had prior and during establishment of a friendship, you'll most likely lose that person as a friend or take a lesser role in that person's life. In any event, it will still derail you from configuring that individual's mind and meeting your goals. This is why once entry to the host's core is gained, you must remain steadfast on interacting with them on a soulful level and avoid the pitfalls of knocking them off cloud nine!

As with any strong plan, the only time you should change its core components is when you see room for improvement. For example, upgrading a budding potential host from conversation at the job to inviting them to your house, from offering coffee to offering an afterhours drink at a bar, from talking about movies to offering to go and see one, from talking about music to offering to go see a concert live, etc.

Remember, configuration is slow methodical processes so keep in mind we are not saying once entry to the soul is granted throw all your cards on the table at once, absolutely not! What we are saying is that the consistency in maintaining soulful interactions is instrumental in configuring somebody's mind once access to their core has been granted. There's no room for complacency when you are trying to configure somebody's mind or maintaining it! This is why you should deploy configuration upon immediate notice of a person going out of their way to harm or help your situation.

Now remember we said the (when) is coupled with (how)! So how do you gain configuration once access to the soul has been granted? Simply put, it is a compilation of all the factual intelligence you have gained over a period of time through various mediums. These mediums can include you, other people's intel on the potential host, the host's actions, etc. For example, let's say you are still in a cordial stage with a potential host and overhear through another person that your potential host likes a particular music artist. If you have determined that this person (who) has something you need to obtain a goal (what) and (why), you will want to use your (interpersonal skills) next time you have a cordial interaction with this individual about that music artist.

It can be a bullshit conversation about something you factually dug up on the artist online or whatever, but the point here is you want to come off as authentic as possible whether you like the artist or not. Remember, you have to play politics! Now, hopefully this conversation, along with other cordial conversations you deploy off the facts you dug up on your potential host, will lead you to the pearly gates of their soul in due time! Then once access has been granted (when) that's when you deploy the (how) you are going to plant your will in this person's mind.

In this scenario, one way would be to graduate the host from cordially talking about their favorite artist to the soulful interaction of inviting them to see the artist in concert (how). Then if everything is going as planned, the host too should start reciprocating such actions that go in your favor of interests as well. Understand this, once reciprocation is deployed equally without prompting, then you are in a good place for configuration! Remember, "Fight fire with fire," reciprocation, and soulful interaction only once this level has been achieved in configuration!

So then over a period of time, if all these principles are met, you can really start hitting on your true agenda all while maintaining the soulful interactions that got you to this point of course (don't go from sugar to shit)! You still want to go about your true agenda in a methodical approach, i.e. testing the water by throwing out hints, steering them without directly putting them where you want them to be, testing them to see how much they value you, etc. If everything is going well and you feel as though you have reached a point where you can lay the foundation of your will in somebody's mind, at this point the trigger should be they haven't told you no on many or any of your requests at all.

You see, once you've gotten someone to the point where it's hard for them to deny you anything, you have successfully configured their mind to align with your interest. The only thing you need to do now is upload your agenda into their mind, ensuring it's not detrimental to their core, and maintain configuration moving forward. Simple as it sounds, it is extremely difficult to obtain. Nevertheless, it is important, I'll even say essential, that you do it because interaction with other humans is undoubtedly the most important skill you'll ever have to learn. It plays an important role in your overall well-being mentally and physically. This is why you can't remain stagnant in your approach to configure brains.

Understand this; it has to be done in order to maintain your sanity and happiness throughout your lifetime! This is why there is no room for regression when configuring other human's minds. As we learned from the first book, regression is a horrible thought process that derails you from achieving your goals of a prosperous life. Since successfully dealing with other humans is vital to your prosperity, you must defeat regression from keeping you from configuring other people's minds! Let's dwell on regression!

Chapter 6: Regression

As we dwell on the aspects of defeating regression as it pertains to configuring other's minds, it is with the upmost importance that we learn to curve the enemy mindset of emotional and subjective abuse (opinions)! Again, this should already be established from the first book, but if it isn't, you'll have to master the art of suppression when it comes to these two antagonists. Hence, you won't be able to pursue configuring someone's mind if you have failed to refrain from being driven by these two major forces. These two entities will primarily be the focus on how not to become a victim of regression while trying to configure someone's mind.

Here are the issues most people face when trying to configure somebody's mind. First of all, you can't let your mind become discouraged when deploying configuration. You have to believe in everything that you are doing in order to achieve the results you desire. This is actually for everything you do in your life! Wise man once said, "Don't do it if your heart is not in it!" This rule of thumb couldn't be truer because it places emphasis on how regression is able to penetrate one's mind, breed in one's mind, and ultimately infest one's mind! This is how a single dose of discouragement from not being able to configure one person's mind could affect you from not ever trying it again! This is truly detrimental to your well-being as you need cooperation of others in this world to obtain your goals.

For example, how many times have you heard someone say, "All men just want is sex and nothing more, or all women just want money and nothing more?" You see, the people who have embedded this ideology in their minds have become subjected to regression via emotions and an opinionated mindset. You see, they may have come in contact with love interests that didn't work out for whatever reason and this is an emotional rationale for why they can't sustain a relationship. You see, as we learned from the first book, you should already have configured your own mind properly. Therefore, you should already know what you are looking for in terms of a love interest as it is aligned with your core values, right!

Second, you should also know what to look out for that could be detrimental to those values before you allow yourself to get hurt. Remember folks everything is intertwined from the first book to this one! The only exception is that here, you are trying to configure somebody else's mind who is a foreign entity of your own. Keep in mind that nobody comes out the pussy preprogrammed to kiss your ass! You have to configure them to do so. Thus, as mentioned just previously, those who short change themselves by categorizing any group of people for any reason will most certainly lose out on a lot in life. For instance, the woman who sees all men just wanting sex has allowed the process of regression to start its infestation.

First of all, with that ideology (penetrating phrase) the woman will become leery of companionship, have trust issues, or may even refrain from a relationship altogether, which we know all are not healthy solutions! Second, this ideology usually hits the second phase of an embedded (opinionated) thought process. What happens is the emotional and opinionated mindset has now driven the woman to relax her standards, come off her core, have trust issues, try to force sustainability, and much more. Lastly, if this ideology is still left unchecked, it will take over her mind (infestation) and dictate to her that this is the standard and it can't get any better, live with it!

The art of configuration can't have this type of thought process in order to work. You see once you have let these three phrases kick in, you're gone! There is no way you can possibly configure somebody's mind because you no longer have faith in what you are doing. As we mentioned earlier in the book, configuration is a slow and methodical process, and no matter what, you must stay persistent in trying to configure key players in your life in order to obtain goals.

You see, as we mentioned also, you are not going to be able to configure everybody but you should either reach a peaceful coexistence or move on to the next. But the key is you don't lose faith in what you are trying to accomplish. You see, in our love interest example the woman lost all faith that she could find the right man to her standards. Here's the kicker to configuration and that is we just mentioned that nobody comes out the womb preprogrammed to kiss your ass! We got to hold true to practicing what we preach, (consistency). At the same time, what if one of those guys who the woman encountered under her prejudice thoughts of just wanting sex could have become the man of her dreams with a little configuration, huh? This is why patience is a virtue in this arena! Let's dwell on this for moment.

Two of the main reasons why some people fail to configure someone else's mind are due to emotions and the opinionated mindset. You see, far too often what happens is that a person allows their configuration process to be derailed by a mere spark of doubt, face value of a word, anger, happiness, and more. To put it bluntly as we mentioned before, you have to have thick skin in order to be able to configure people. For example, Jesus, Dr. Martin Luther King, Jr., and Ben Franklin all were once criticized for their beliefs, yet to this very day, their ideals play major roles in the functionality of society today.

Think about that for a minute! What if Dr. King stopped preaching for love and unity due to his critics? Do you think the minds he was able to configure in the name of righteousness would have happened and continue to happen to this day? What if Ben Franklin would have stopped working on his inventions due to his critics? Would we have the level of technology that we currently enjoy today or the motivation he has configured in the minds of all inventors after him creating new innovation for mankind? What if Jesus stopped his messages due to criticism? Would we have a worldwide religion that governs millions of people and continues to inspire people to this day?

You see, this is configuration. You're not always going to see results immediately. Rather your goal is to see people aligned with your ideals for the long term, and your configuration has the ability to bring new people in via the people you have already configured or with the consistent success of a configuration program. This is why you must have thick skin and roll with the punches to see your configuration through.

Look at what these historical figures would have lost out on had they retired their ideals! There's no place for regression during configuration rather, as the first book taught us, there's no place for regression period in your life! Here's an example of how people fail to configure due to lack of waterproof skin. I'll use one of my own life's lessons as an example.

I remember back in 8th grade, my second go round at it (SMH). I got left back (LOL); now I'm a fucking author, go figure (SMH). I was approached by this girl who wanted to be my girlfriend. She was by society standards obese but fairly attractive. I was criticized by the male and female peers within my circle for even thinking about entertaining the girl's offer of a relationship. You see she was also deemed a nerd and typically hung out with the so-called unpopular kids! I was still developing myself as a person but I still had an understanding of this girl's future potential for me. However, I wasn't yet strong enough to withstand the barrage of insults that where surely to come my way if everyone knew I was dating this girl.

Therefore, like a spineless coward, I choose to ignore the girl's advances and even became ignorant towards her in order to keep my so to speak, cool status with the "in crowd." It hurt me inside because it was never in my DNA to treat anyone foul without probable cause, but my lack of core, foundation, and opinionated mindset drove me to drastic measures. Accordingly, my flawed plan worked and she ceased to deal with me. Keep in mind I said (flawed) plan! You see, although I was successful in eliminating someone detrimental to my coolness, my actions would come back to bite me in the ass later, as you will soon find out!

So, time went on and I eventually dropped out of school altogether. No dreams, no job, diving in unhealthy relationships, no goals, and then one day upon entering this business establishment, I see this girl who I made an enemy of several years prior. She looked fantastic! She had loss the weight and was dressed in a professional manner. Oh (BTW) I still would have fucked her when she was fat. It was just peer pressure driving me not to, just wanted to throw that out there (LOL)! I walked up to her and said, "Hey how are, do you remember me?" She shrugged her head as if to say, "Fuck out of here!" I couldn't tell whether she remembered me and was like fuck me for the ignorance I conveyed to her back in the day, or she couldn't remember and wasn't feeling the stranger in her presence! I just walked it off and looked back at her one more time in awe of what could have been!

I wasn't worth shit at this time so you can imagine how my awe was times 10 at this point in my life. I never saw her again in my life to this day, but I did around that time after that incident manage to run into one of her close friends she had back in school. I told her about my encounter with her old buddy and she replied, "Yeah, I know she told me she saw your ass, and you were trying to say hi to her!" I said, "Damn, so she really did know who I was!" She replied, "Yeah, she said she wasn't thinking about you." Again, in my head I was like damn because, for one I deserved it because of the way I treated her; and two, the mistake I made years ago was biting me in the ass.

I inquired about her life and her friend told me that she was currently married to a businessman, she graduated from college, was the vice president of the corporation I saw her at, drives a nice expensive automobile, and owned a beachfront property. Again, I thought my, my, my, what could have been? I left the conversation at that and told her friend to tell her old buddy I was proud of her and much success to her in the future. I felt that was the least I can do to try and make amends for the devious things I done in the past and hopefully try to spark a friendship in the future if our paths were ever to cross again.

You see, I lost configuration back in the day due to emotions and an opinionated mindset. Look at all I lost! First of all, I lost a chance of marrying a beautiful and intelligent woman. Second, think about the trickle-down effect. With her by my side even as just a friend, I might have never dropped out of school with her motivation and help. At the same time, she could have employed me at her company when I so desperately needed cash! She could have been a reference for me for buying a house, a mentor for obtaining a corporate job like hers, or just a plain old good friend with all the benefits that derive from that (get your minds out the gutter I do mean platonic friends in a scenario we weren't dating). In a nutshell, my life could have turned out in a completely different manner for the good earlier than it did! That is what I lost due to my inability to configure her at the time. You see even though her weight wasn't an issue for me at the time, if it was her wishes, I could have help configured her mind to lose weight. A simple thing to do in consideration to all that I lost.

As I mentioned before, you don't want to be in the realm of (what) if! You see, due to my failed attempt at configuration, I was left to think what if I would have silenced the noise from my critics and configured that young woman to be my girl? By the way, most of the critics back then aren't doing as well. In fact, some have even died from self-afflictions! This is what regression does to you when you are trying to configure someone else's mind. It sinks you into depression even further if your emotions are running amuck already. You see the key here is I didn't know what this young lady was going to become back then. Hell, I didn't know what I was going to become, let alone her! Despite not knowing the unknown, I did however know something about her. I noticed she was intelligent way back then already. Even if I didn't know her future, her intelligence at the very least gave me a glimmer of what was forthcoming in her life. The configuration would have been just to foster that and hopefully that would have aided me in becoming a better person in one shape or another! Again, look what I had stood to gain!

Keep in mind the peaceful coexistence policy is in effect here too (intertwined) because even without her vagina, I could have still enjoyed a cordial friendship hadn't I deployed a flawed plan (ignorance and divide). This is losing configuration and how it can come back and bite you square on your ass if you let the components of regression invade your mind! So, what you must understand is that you can't be deterred by the attitude of your host or by those in your inner circle. You have to come to a realization that what you are doing by way of configuration will aid you in some capacity of your life if not all of it. This will stem from prioritizing goals set by your core and foundation, of course.

You see, had I prioritized my future well-being over some peer pressure, I would have possibly married a dynamic woman. Take this powerful notion for thought: every decision you have ever made that impacted you for good or worse was directly or indirectly influenced by another human. This is why it is so important to have your mind configured first prior to configuring others!

Rule of thumb here folks, is that when you know what you are configuring for, you are least likely to have it derailed by a lesser priority in your life. You can't avoid other humans no matter how hard you try folks. It's going to happen! You have to be ready to configure at all times and at all costs. Food for thought here is you never know who you might need! Now with that said keep in mind that it's not all about the uplifting folks in your life, it's also about the Debbie Downers as well. They too must be configured to a peaceful coexistence or hopefully altogether configured to your goals! The impact of your antagonist can be felt just as deep as your protagonist. As much as we would like to see haters go away, they are here to stay!

Think about this for a minute, most people can't coexist with their enemy. Do you possess the ability to coexist with your enemy? If you don't, then you have lost the battleground on configuring somebody else's mind! The perceived enemy can knock you off your foundation just as quickly as you can impose it on yourself. However, I want you to notice how I describe the antagonist as a perceived enemy. Remember, you can learn a lot from every walk of life on this planet and that notion pertains to those aligned or not aligned to your goals. Moreover, if you allow such a prejudiced mindset to corupt your system, the emotional component will most surely imbed itself within your mind next.

This is the process that happens when people can't coexist with their enemies. They allow the emotional justification of repelling any type of relationship with that person due to the perception or fact of how they feel about them. Wise man summed it up so elegantly when he or she said, "Keep your friends close and your enemies even closer!" Understand the ideology behind this quote. For example, let's say you are trying to configure a coworker's mind to performing at a high level to make your job easier. Then let's say for whatever reason that coworker resisted your efforts of configuration and proceeded to try and make your life hell. They can try to do this in numerous ways of course but just for this example, let's say they complained to the supervisor that you were harassing them about their performance and you are not their boss! Now let's say your supervisor is involved and now investigating the allegations brought forth from your co-worker about your unprofessional behavior.

What subsequent repercussions do you think are going to follow next? Here goes that replay ladies and gents! Everything is intertwined together, right to obtain your goals! Let's analyze this antagonist situation here. First of all, if the supervisor is a true manager at their core then that means that no employee under his or her responsibility should be slacking. Accordingly, the manager would need everyone to work at highly efficient levels in order for the supervisor to look good and maintain their employment, right! That should be at the core of every manager's mindset.

Therefore, from the onset, using the scientific method, your hypothesis should have been that the manager obviously is deficient in getting this particular employee to perform for whatever reason. I want you to take notice of how I worded that statement. I said obviously deficient in getting this particular employee to perform, not all of them. Why's this so important? This is important because you can't have tunnel vision while configuring somebody else's mind. Remember, as I eluded just a few sentences ago, everything is intertwined and you have to be objective about your approach always. As it pertains to this example, objectivity is how do you know the manager is actually deficient in evaluating the performance of this particular coworker? There is nothing wrong with the hypothesis but you just want to broaden the horizon of it to help obtain a concrete resolution to the issue after the experiment. Remember, configuration of others is a slippery slope because you don't know who is trying to configure who and who is trying to configure you! Think about this!

What if the reason the manager isn't on this coworker because they have already configured the manager to let them slack off for whatever reason? What if the coworker and supervisor are dating? You might not be aware of this but obviously that can possibly spell disaster for you. What if the coworker has a similar claim against the supervisor and he or she is scared to confront the employee over fear of losing their job? What if the manager is letting the employee off easy in order to obtain something of value from that employee? That can be a multitude of things within itself but whatever it is, it can be important enough to have you become a causality of their war of configuring the slacking coworker's mind!

Now take this into consideration. Your perception of this coworker as being an enemy due to the fact he or she is making your life difficult at work has now become a battle of configuring two minds, not just one! Keep in mind as well that one of the individuals holds your financial well-being in their hands! Moreover, you still haven't determined who else is aligned with the manager and coworker, just the coworker, or just the manager. I'm only saying two people for this example but the law of configuration states that you aren't just configuring the mind of the particular host but all who will come in contact with that person as well. Who knows how many antagonists you have unleashed upon you with your actions! Keep in mind there could be some protagonists in there too, including the manager, but you should always plan for the unforeseen, right!

Remember unforeseen circumstances are highly relevant to regression invading your mindset and you losing configuration especially to a perceived enemy. You have to at least coexist with them so long as their actions aren't extremely detrimental to your core and foundation. Remember if there is at least a peaceful coexistence, this still keeps the door open to possible alignment down the road! You see there is nothing wrong with determining that somebody is making your job more difficult than it has to be if you did so under the lens of objectivity. However, there is something wrong with disliking them because of it even if they are doing it intentionally. This type of antagonist also goes by the name of asshole, just an FYI!

You see, we started off with that wise man quote of keeping thy enemy close, right. Here's why. Separating

83

yourself from the action, whether good or bad, is detrimental to configuration. In other words, you need to continuously engage those who are opposed or supportive of your mindset in order to know what they are thinking. You need to be able to manipulate, prevent, or prepare for their next attack in order to keep the supportive folks aligned with you and the negative folks held at bay from knocking you off your core and foundation.

Think about this! Every country on this planet has spies that keep an eye on other nations. These are countries that are allied and especially those that are enemies of each other. Rationale is that you can't afford to not know what is coming or being planned! You need a person, machine, or a combination on the inside in order to ascertain critical information that can benefit your goals. It is almost impossible to obtain such knowledge through distance other than a computer and even still the crucial aspect of human to human dialogue, body language, and physical interaction will be omitted from the data collection. This plays a crucial role in painting the full picture.

For example, let's get back to our coworker scenario and possible reasons the manager is allowing him or her to slack. We said for one they might be shacking up, right. So, let us say you were able to infiltrate the manager's files and found that the employee hasn't been disciplined for poor performance. Your hypothesis states in part that the employee is slacking off due to a lack of manager scrutiny. The (who) is allowing your coworker other than themselves to perform so poorly, right? However, the picture isn't clear yet.

Remember, who, what, when, why, and how factor applies to analytical situations! We need to discover the reason (why) the manager is allowing such detrimental behavior to their own well-being. This is when analyzing that human interaction becomes crucial to painting the full picture of who you are trying to configure. Files don't confirm somebody is dating. The files only confirm that the person hasn't been disciplined because the manager has been reluctant to do so for whatever reason. Now if you see the manager always around the coworker, suspect physical interaction, and possible dialogue that suggests a deeper relationship than normal work environment protocol, now you can start to paint the picture of what's going on!

Keep in mind it has to be based off fact before you render judgement but even if the relationship isn't sexual in nature, a friendship, a sibling, in-law, or department snitch (LOL) type relationship is still enough ammunition to outline your rules of engagement to configuration. You see the rules will undoubtedly change given the nature of the relationship coupled with your findings in the manger's file. You having this information now may make you hesitant to talk to the employee about their performance as you had originally done because if their relationship is that strong with the supervisor, nine out of 10 times there isn't shit the manager is going to do about it. Hence, they weren't doing anything about it in the first place, and second if the relationship is proven, then you more than likely will become the target in order to protect the alignment the manager and coworker have.

As we said, now keep in mind that there is nothing wrong with having a goal of making your life easy at work by trying to configure this antagonist. You just need to know what you are up against and how you should approach it. Key word here is approach not run away! Understand that the goal that you set forth must be achieved one way or another, and failure is not an option. You are just going to have to work hard at it but keep insight that some way somehow configuration will happen! So instead of refraining from interaction with this antagonist knowing the uphill battle you face, now is the time to patronize their mind more so than you were going to originally. The reason is obviously to reach your goals of a better work environment.

You see, people separate from their enemies through tunnel vison and say this is never going to work but that is not always the case. In fact, if people weren't so premature in dissolving relationships, there would be a lot less people in the world crying over lost opportunity! Let's get back to the world nations and how each spy on the other. Let's use the nations who are enemies. For example, let us say the reason for conflict is nuclear power. Then let us say that one nation dominates the other because of its military capabilities. The nation that is being dominated doesn't have nuclear capability but wishes to do so to protect its country from bullying.

Now let's say the bullied nation is using the laws of configuring the minds of others by applying the wise man theory of keeping your enemies close. You see much like the bullied nation, you are being taken advantage of at work due to the arsenal your coworker has in their pocket, namely your supervisor. Now let's say instead of upsetting their antagonist (the nuclear power), they patronized the nation with numerous liaisons and aligned themselves with the nuclear power's goals. Then let's say through strategic planning, the bullied nation was able to ascertain the blueprints on how to build a nuclear bomb from the nuclear power and over time became a nuclear power all on their own. Now that the nation being bullied has achieved this platform, they begin to uphold their core values and foundation pushing back on the nation that has bullied them for years.

You see they essentially kept their enemy close in order to obtain the necessary information needed to either defeat them or maintain a peaceful coexistence! It would have been difficult to do this if the bullied nation always bickered with the nuclear power and strained the relationship. You see the bullied nation knew the nuclear power was an antagonist to its core values and foundation but given the arsenal the nuclear power had, it would have been practically suicidal to let their true aspirations be known at a point when they were inferior. The nuclear power if known of their intentions could have disrupted the progress through a multitude of ways, such as embargos, barring their citizens into their nation, tightening security so it's not stolen, and more. This obviously took time for the bullied nation to accomplish in this example but the key here is they didn't break configuration even knowing the nuclear power was an enemy to the country.

The same applies to the coworker scenario. By keeping the antagonist coworker close, there can be a multitude of avenues you can use to obtain your goal. You already know they aren't aligned with your goals but you don't treat them as such. Configure their mind! Some possible outcomes could be the coworker actually befriending you and start doing their fair share workload to appease your budding friendship. Your coworker could also tell your supervisor positive things about you because of the friendship, and the manager starts allowing you to slack. You could gather information that can support your case of favoritism and get the manager and coworker removed. You could learn how to configure the manager too through friendship with the coworker and much more.

The key here is to keep objectivity open and refrain from tunnel vision of a lost situation. Keep in mind here that the situation should be extremely detrimental in order for you to go to the extreme of having someone excluded from your life. As the laws of configuration tell us, you never know who you might need in this lifetime. It is more conducive to your health to have friends not enemies. You will have to judge the situation accordingly, but however you map out the plan, it should remain steadfast until your goal of configuration is met and you obtained the enrichment you sought after. You can only do that with consistency. You see if you were to give up all hope of configuring your coworker, you would without a doubt stay unhappy in the situation which could cause stress and other issues, up to losing your job! Regression as alluded to in the first book, will never invade your mind if you just stay focused on the light at the end of the tunnel. Let's dwell on consistently configuring other's minds!

Chapter 7: Consistency

The ability to persevere is usually taught, not inherited contrary to popular belief. All humans are born with some type of breaking point! Everybody has that threshold when they just say, "All right, fuck it, I've had enough!" There's nothing in essence wrong with this notion. However, at the same time, you have to teach yourself that once you have reached your boiling point, you don't allow that to derail you from your plan of configuration. Think about this for a second. If Dr. Martin Luther King, Jr. would have said fuck it and turned to violence instead of a nonviolent philosophy, where would history and his legacy stand today? Think about it. We are all human. You don't think for one minute he didn't get upset after all that abuse and mistreatment he received! Yet, he remained dedicated to configuring the minds of politicians, racists, and his followers to his ideals of equality. He never wavered, but what if he allowed himself to do so?

You see, again, there's nothing wrong with reaching a boiling point so long as it is balanced with the principles of a plan and the (when) factor! Keep in mind the boiling point, under the plan implementation principle, becomes a time limitation on when your plan isn't getting results. Thus, it's time to reevaluate and develop a new strategy to get to your goal. It doesn't mean that you say fuck it and give up. It means you say fuck it and reconstruct. Keep in mind, no matter how monumental the task may seem, you have to see it through to the end or reach a peaceful coexistence. Don't stop no matter what.

Here's the beauty of configuring other's minds. Remember we stated that you are not only configuring the mind of the person you are trying to align to your goals but you are also configuring that person to configure all of those who they interact with on your behalf. You see that's the residual importance of configuration. You never know what you are walking away from when you say fuck it! Even though it seems you'll never ever be able to configure a particular individual, you never know for one who's watching, who's listening, who's interested, who that person has actually gained you an ally vicariously, etc.

For example, let's use Dr. Martin Luther King, Jr. again here. Let's say, Dr. King wasn't able to configure a certain politician's mind, but through sheer perseverance, he was able to configure the mind of a loved one to the politician. Then let's say that loved one was able to configure the mind of the politician Dr. King couldn't initially break through. Now more than likely, that once seemingly impenetrable politician now will try and configure the mind of his or her colleagues. Then if success with at the very least one colleague, then that person will more than likely start the same chain reaction to all who he or she interacts with. You see the beauty of that!

Now for a moment let's play devil's advocate. Let's say Dr. King took the fuck it approach and then changed his philosophy to violence. We already know that the politician wasn't aligned with Dr. King but what about his or her loved one? You see the loved one could have started out as a supporter of the politician's ideals but saw Dr. King's nonviolent approach as ideology that all mankind could benefit from. You see that is a gateway for Dr. King's message to infect this host and begin laying the grassroots for configuration. Now keep in mind, all of this would be unknowing to Dr. King. However, it is his consistency in thought that eventually he will persuade the masses to advocate equality. Thus, he never says fuck it and closes the door!

Now as we are continuing to play devil's advocate, if Dr. King takes the violent route, this would turn the once potential host to a firm antagonist to Dr. King's cause. Dr. King essentially lost configuration due to inconsistency. All because he said, "Fuck it," due to the seemingly inability to configure the main host he desired, he has now made his cause that much more difficult to achieve. Remember, patience is a virtue! Keep ramming the message home despite how the odds may stack up.

Remember wise man once said, "Where there's a will, there's a way!" Understand that to the essence of your core! The best way to remain consistent is to never become stagnant in your approach. As we mentioned several times already, there's more than one way to skin a cat! If you set your core and foundation correctly as per the guidelines and principles from the first book, you should be able to easily diversify yourself under the same core and foundation from which you stand.

For example, Dr. King's nonviolent approach didn't stop at just displaying brilliant resilience via verbal, physical, and mental abuse of the antagonist of his time. No, no, no, he expanded on the core of nonviolence and stood on the foundation of not fighting violence with violence by branching off those respective tree branches.

Remember the tree principle from plan implementation in the first book? Everything is intertwined folks, reminder number 100! Under the core and foundation of non-violence, Dr. King also instituted such tactics as boycotting, delivering speeches, staging marches, writing politicians, ministering, educating peers, and much more. All of these avenues were instrumental in achieving the main objective of gaining equal rights! All were still under the core and foundation from which Dr. King set for him first, and then he passed it on to the masses.

Keep this as a rule of thumb, that the more options you give yourself, the better chance you have of obtaining a goal. Diversify, diversify, and diversify! If you were to ask many successful entrepreneurs, they would tell you that it is highly improbable that your first idea is going to be your meal ticket! Even if it is, you still need to consistently reinvent your model to stay relevant and withstand competition. Moreover, you still need to invest in other areas in case this idea eventually fails. If you analyze some of the most successful companies, you would be amazed at the diverse industries they are invested in deviating from the core business. Same principles here folks, just applied to different aspects in life but yet they work across the board!

We mentioned earlier in this book that it is crucial that you deploy numerous tactics to invade your host and configure their mind. Through the scientific method, you should already have prior to trying to configure the host's mind, have an educated guess (hypothesis) on what it may take to configure the host's mind, a reason for why you are configuring the host's mind (state the problem or need), conduct an experiment (you deploying numerous tactics to see if configuration can be achieved), through consistency (analyzing) the data from the experiment to see how well the configuration is going as it pertains to enriching you, or learning from the data the necessary changes needed to reconstruct your plans of configuration (reflection).

The process doesn't change until configuration is achieved, not achieved, or maintained. You just keep recycling the process regardless! Think about this for a moment. Most people usually reach their boiling points due to fatigue. In other words, they are tired of fighting and getting nowhere or have just become flat out complacent. Whatever is the predominant factor, there's no place for it in your mind or the mind of who you are trying to configure. Point blank, period! This hinders consistency and in the worst-case scenarios, kills it altogether. The system of configuring the human mind through the core of humanology is designed as such to resist fatigue. You just have to trust in the system! You won't suffer from fatigue unless you fail to adhere to the principles from *The Core of Humanology and How to Configure the Human Mind*.

Think about it for moment. When you first learn how to drive there are some bumps in the road, right. You're learning how to measure braking distances in different weather conditions, parallel parking, signage, directions on the roads, etc. Then after a few years on the road (consistently), driving becomes second nature. In the beginning you were apprehensive about making tight turns, parking in tight spots, and parallel parking, and now it comes as natural as breathing. You don't even think about it; rather you are now driving on sheer instincts and your abilities have transcended from being taught, to learned, and then to being automatic.

Same principles here folks again just another aspect of life, yet it works through consistency. It was the same way through configuring other folk's minds. It is usually rough when trying to get to know a person initially. Although strong interpersonal skills help break barriers down quickly, it can still be a challenge. However, once you deploy the scientific method and experiment with what works and what doesn't work with a person, it should gradually become easier to configure that person's mind, or at least give you an inclination of the path you should take forward to achieve your goal.

Obviously if you're keeping up with the principles, this is where you are going to reconstruct or enhance plans of configuration. Remember, we just mentioned you continuously recycle these methods until your goal is achieved, but every time you recycle it, keep in mind you are getting better and better. You want to get to the point of what's learned of the person by them teaching you through their actions, and words become innate in your mind on how to handle them.

Once this is achieved, now it's just a war of minds and who will outlast the other. Whereas fatigue is the antagonist to consistency, stamina is the protagonist to it. Sheer will and determination ultimately will determine who wins the configuration of minds. In conjunction with that, you should reasonably assume that it is possible that no matter how strong willed they may seem in rebuking your configuration, they may be wearing down over time. Also consume this food for thought. Everybody isn't going to possess the skill of configuration either for their own mind or others. Therefore, I'll put my configured mind of humanology to battle an unconscious human mind any day of the week consistently. I like my chances and so should you!

You see, as we speak on stamina and how it is such a protagonist to consistency, the core reason being is the conditioning of the mind! A well configured mind is set to stand the test of a lifetime. It is durable and highly resistant to virus. Wise man once said, "You have a brain but you don't have a mind!" Once you configure your mind, its conditioning aids you in maintaining consistency. An unconscious mind blind to the principles of the core of humanology is unconditioned. It is vulnerable to parasitic thought processes and generally doesn't possess the stamina to withstand the trauma of life.

This is why a lot of people come to despise mathematics. Addition and subtraction are easy but when you get to the complexity of calculus, that's when people generally fall off. Their mind isn't conditioned enough to get to an answer that is vague and requires multiple steps in order to get a resolution. They essentially say, "Fuck It! I'll find a career that doesn't require a strong concentration in math." Hence, that's why we generally have a shortage of workers needed in mathematically driven fields.

Understand this word fatigue. What does it mean at the core as it pertains to the brain? Think about it a second.

It's scientific fact that the muscles of the body need rest after being exhausted through physical activity. Last checked you don't do any heavy lifting directly with your brain. Therefore, how can it suffer from fatigue? I know you hear the same ole' clichés like, "I need a mental break," or "This is weighing heavy on my mind!" All that is utter bullshit with a capital "B"! Again, I have to ask, how does a brain that isn't involved with any physical activity suffer from fatigue? Oh, and by the way, those clichés spoken by individuals should heighten your configuration senses as strong possible candidates for invasion; hence, their mind is obviously lacking stamina.

Fatigue in the mind is a virus and the strongest antagonist of them all. You see people who say "Fuck It" have failed to configure their minds properly and therefore have allowed detrimental thought processes to take up residency in their brain (virus). You see it is impossible for the brain to become fatigued in the objective sense of the word. It is however possible for somebody who hasn't configured their mind to conjure up an excuse for their lack of brain stamina! Let's dwell on the core meaning of fatigue in the brain. Let's discuss once again the juggernaut called an emotion and how it places severe strain on configuring the minds of others.

Chapter 8: Emotion

Ahhh, those pesky emotions. They never fail to misguide us, huh? However, you should now possess the ability to suppress emotions at this point, but if you haven't, I suggest you put this book down and read the first book before attempting the configuration of others. As we alluded to in the previous chapter, configuring someone's mind practically takes a lifetime! I would say marathon but that would give you the illusion that configuration will eventually have an ending, and quite frankly it doesn't. Now with that said obviously it would take a lifetime of stamina to maintain or obtain configuration of another's mind. This is why it is essential that you maintain your mental stability for configuring others to your goals. You cannot under any means allow fatigue to fester in your mind.

Keep in mind as you grow, your goals should grow along with that growth. Thus, it may be necessary to reconfigure, maintain current configuration, or configure a person who you've already configured. For example, let's say you successfully configured your spouse's mind to allow you to quit work and go back to school to acquire the education you desire. Now accordingly, let's say you graduate and find employment in your new career path. At the same time, your mind is simultaneously gravitating in using your new career down the road to entrepreneurship. Understand now it already takes a considerable amount of effort and understanding that your spouse has already conformed to in order for you to realize your first goal. Now, you are pushing the envelope for that same person you configured already to now adjust and conform to new goals! Look, if the person is fully onboard with you, that's fine but also note it is extremely rare! With that said, in most cases, your goals aren't going to be the goals of others you are trying to configure.

Just as this chapter is teaching you how to resist fatigue, you must also instill in your host how to resist fatigue of aiding you in your goals! Easily said but difficult to obtain! Understand this, it's one thing for you to get your host to configure to one objective, but more and more gets tricky! For instance, how many couples you heard broke up because one or both parties changed and it wasn't what one or both parties expected the relationship to be? That sum of those two parts of the equation usually equals the quote, "We just fell apart!" If you're married the sum of the equation is "irreconcilable differences!" Hopefully you can stick to the "we just fell apart" version because the irreconcilable differences are going to cost your ass more! Just saying!

Understand the underlying issue here, one or both parties ceased to adhere to the other's goal. In essence of it all, configuration was lost. Now using this theory and applying it to our example, the spouse may have signed on to their significant other educating themselves to enhance personal enrichment, but they may resent what business ownership might bring. They may resent the long hours it may take to develop the business. They may resent putting up the finances necessary to start or maintain the business. Their emotions may prompt them to resent what wealth may influence on the relationship, etc. This is just the tip of the iceberg here folks, but the idea here is as your goals change so does the reconfiguration, maintaining the configuration thereof, or newly configuring your host's mind.

Follow me here folks, when you ask your spouse to now reconfigure their mind from education to business, you are asking them to adjust to more time devoted to business, paperwork, finance, risk, their time, support, understanding, and much more! When you ask your spouse to configure their mind from education to business as it pertains to maintaining the current state of configuration, you are asking them to adhere to lesser time spent with each other, more finances, more of their time, more understanding, more support, etc. When you ask your spouse to configure their mind from education to business in the essence of a newly configured path, you are saying, ok the education was cool but I want more!

Keep in mind even though we separated these details of configuration, they still work in cohesion. What we are doing as we are separating reconfiguration, maintaining configuration, and configuring is that in certain situations, you may be able to get away with just deploying one of those stages. However, for preventative measures and as the first book teaches you, it's always good practice to plan for unforeseen circumstances. Thus, it pays to deploy all stages to ensure a solid configuration from there and beyond. Remember everything works interwoven and the principles of the first book still apply here folks!

The best tool that you can deploy when it comes to configuring someone's mind is the authenticity of you. That only comes as you know yourself and desires which is the dialogue of the first publication. You see, it's not that farfetched to seek new alliances to your new goals from your spouse if they see the fruits of their help. Remember the principles of reciprocation and action here! Talking a good game and your actions prove null and void could easily hasten one's retreat from you or slowly erode trust, all of which will ultimately hinder or abort configuration altogether.

Getting back to our example as it pertains to our principles here, you give yourself a better chance of reconfiguring, maintaining configuration, or configuring by showing and proving. For example, wouldn't you be more likely to lend someone money who always repaid as they say they would? So just think for a moment that even if it's unknowing about how your spouse may feel about you entering the world of business, if you have shown the reciprocation of graduating, shouldering the burden of finances once you were employed, supporting your spouse's desires, rededicating time to your spouse, etc., this may relax their apprehension of supporting you in endeavors foreign or already aligned with a current path.

Now on the other hand, if your spouse sees that you have failed at obtaining the education you sought, financial burden still remains, etc., it's just reasonable to assume they may not fully or support at all future cause in this particular area or other areas. You see, expanding on reciprocation is not only the aspect of giving back what you have received, it's also the reward of dedication. It was a team effort that allotted you to obtain a goal of education and ultimately employment. Understand when someone is configured to your goal and more importantly you configured them right, your goals should be just as personal to them as it is to you! Therefore, when you fail, they also feel the brunt of failure. On the other hand, they also feel the jubilation of success that the partnership of your goal came to fruition.

How many people you know said they helped someone, and after the person got what they wanted from them they kicked them to the curb! Take that same scenario and ask yourself of those people, how many said the individual came back begging for help again! Continue with that scenario, and get the percentage of those who were taken advantage of who said they would never fuck with that asshole again. Everything is interwoven folks; you never know who you might need!

What we are saying is that you never under any circumstances intentionally break configuration unless the configuration has become toxic to your core and foundation. So, if your spouse isn't emotionless as the first book teaches you to be, or if they are emotional you still must maintain configuration. Remember your goal is their goal so whether the spouse is emotional or not the ripple effects are real. Obviously if the spouse is emotional the situation could get a little stickier than an emotionless individual but repercussions are what they are!

For example, a spouse who's mastered the principle of suppressing emotions will undoubtedly judge on action rather than outcome. What that means is that if you do succeed in obtaining your education and gaining employment, you will be judged on the totality of your actions as they pertain to a relationship (reciprocation). This is the same as if you don't succeed at achieving the education you wanted at first, try because remember you should always persevere and strive until you get what you want because you still will be judged accordingly. Listen, you can't lose configuration regardless.

Again, if you are reading this book, you should be emotionless at this point and the theory is how to control your host's emotions toward you, not the other way around. You can't allow your host to fester feelings of trust erosion because that's a significant barrier to configuration. Even if you have a failed attempt, you have to keep it in your mind that your host, spouse in this scenario, still believes that you will eventually obtain your goal with their assistance. At the same time, if you do succeed you need to ensure your spouse is going to reap the benefits of their labor as well. However the cards may fall, the trick is to keep the door open for future invasions to your host's mind.

I'll say it again, the best way to keep your host's emotions in check is to apply the principles of *The Core of Humanology and How to Configure the Human Mind*, particularly while constructing a good plan of invasion. Just as we stressed earlier in this book, a sound plan is instrumental to getting desirable results. Also, not to say the least, it is just as important to keep your own emotions in check as well. Again, it is what you already should be doing! You need to know that even if your host is displaying an undesirable action against your goal that doesn't mean configuration is all lost. Don't get all perturbed and allow your (emotions) to sway you into thinking configuration can't be achieved or your potential host could possibly derail you.

For instance, let's say you have a spat with your boss at work. Now at the core, your immediate supervisor is the bridge that connects you to food, water, and shelter. This importance is of obvious consequences if lost, right! Think for a second, however! Does one disagreement, spat, write up, or even several disciplinary scenarios warrant you to disengage from configuration? Granted, if it gets to the point of endangering your core and foundation, you should already be planning to remove yourself from that situation, following the principles of the first book. However, if it is minute in nature, you should still pursue configuring your host with urgency, especially if it is an entity that is critical to your core and foundation.

Simply put, many individuals who are criticized by their superiors tend to have a lack of respect for them from there on (emotions) and they lack (objectivity) going forward! This is definitely not the path you want to take while trying to configure someone's mind. Remember as we continuously mention in this book, configuration is a slippery slope but you can't lose sight of the rewards you garner once obtained. Accordingly, keep in mind the reward should always outweigh the risk! That should be a no brainer at this point!

Your configuration of your own mind from the first book should have you looking through the lens of objectivity and being in a stable mindset of being emotionless. Meaning that instead of making a foe out of an essential person you need aligned with you, you would instead through objectivity, take the validity of the discipline the supervisor issued you and try to correct it! Keep it in mind though as long as it's not detrimental to your core and foundation. Don't get it fucked up here! We are well aware that all of your boss's shit doesn't smell like roses! We know that there are plenty of assholes out there, and some people are just plain ignorant with a core of just causing pain!

Even with that scenario, just as I mentioned, you should still be analyzing the situation and start the process of removing yourself from the bullshit. Don't stay there all emotional and fight a liar until that liar disrupts your means of financial stability. You'll be surprised how many people take this route. However, if your mind is configured correctly as it should and has to be, your outlook on this situation should be different.

You see, you need to adhere to that old wise man quote of, "Take a licking and keep on ticking." All negative feedback doesn't meet the criteria of folding, panicking, or relinquishing your potential stake in that person's mind that was critical of you. Again, I use the example of how many of your friends or people you know now hold folk dear to them in their life in which at first they couldn't stand. How many times you had an argument with your brother, sister, mother, father, coworker, boss, girlfriend, boyfriend, wife, kids, and still you are cordially engaged in their life? Think about that for a minute. As angry as you probably were at the time of unrest between one of those entities mentioned, you still somehow remained a part of their life. In other words, you got over it and moved on, if the situation was trivial in nature. You rationalized that it just wasn't worth losing such an important part of your life. Hence, same way you have to look at configuration for the long haul.

Understand this with the upmost clarity, once you strike someone's core, they will become aligned with you in some sort of capacity. It's not guaranteed that you can get their allegiance to all your goals, but definitely a specific area of mutual focus can be achieved. For example, if your boss is analyzed by you properly and through his or her actions can be reasonably assumed as just, (remember you never really truly know someone ever) then you should be able at the very least obtain configuration to common cores of your jobs. Hence, a supervisor needs strong employees to perform in order for the entire department to flourish, which in return, promotes job security for your supervisor. Common sense right! So, if the supervisor is reasonably perceived by you as just, then it should be your rational thought through objectivity that you need to correct your behavior.

Here's the big umbrella, if the department operates efficiently and is effective, that aids you in job security as well, right? So, if that's the case, shouldn't there be some type of cohesion between you and your supervisor to obtain at least this one mutual goal? You can't let your attitude impact your sound principle of reciprocation here. Remember, we mentioned earlier that you must come across to your potential host as an authentic supporter of their goals too in order for configuration to work. You see, if a (just) supervisor finds the need to criticize you on your performance, nine out of ten times it's to protect his or her interest in their financial well-being. Does this make sense?

Moreover, snack on this tidbit of configuration, that not only should you and your boss be in cohesion to make the department look good to maintain employment for all, but you should also be in cohesion to keep perceived just people around you. Meaning you also need to keep in mind that your boss has to answer to someone too, right! So, if you and your coworkers aren't getting the job done that clearly reflects on your boss in which normally doesn't bring favor for his or her superior. Simply put, you know what usually happens next, right? Manager usually gets the axe, no surprise there.

Now there's going to be some folk who might have weathered the storm of discipline and cheered the supervisor's demise but trust me, wise man once said, "They know not what they do!" What can of worms you think the demise of a just boss leads to? Let me give a possible scenario! Nine out of ten times the superior who terminated your boss is going to be looking for a new and improved version, is that fair to say? I'll answer that! You already fucking know! Then what usually happens? Hold on, I'll answer that shit too! You usually end up with a newly hired supervisor who was configured upon hire of the ills of the department and given a set of mandates to achieve in order to remain employed. You don't have to take our words for it, ask around. Anybody who has been through any change of management knows that even if the department is fucked up or a well-oiled machine, there's going to be some bullshit changes coming. Now this new individual could be just or an asshole, but whatever the case, changes are coming that will undoubtedly impact you in some way. With all that said, what would you rather have? A new boss who's possibly an asshole aiming to fire you and others to impress their superior? Or maybe even a just boss who's even sterner than your prior boss who may also fire you? Pick your poison! Whichever scenario you face will bring its own unique challenges.

Remember, the principles remain the same here, that not only are you configuring the host you are trying to infect, you are also configuring vicariously all others that host interacts with as well! So, I want you to take the totality of just this scenario on how emotions not only impact your host in sight but those who the person interacts with as well. Let's get even broader for a second. What if the emotional toll you unleash on your boss is impacting their home life? You ever thought about that? Remember we are talking about humans here, right? You don't think from time to time they talk about their day to their spouse, kids, friends, etc.? What if the spouse sees the impact you are putting on his or her spouse? What do you think they are going to recommend? How do you think his or her kids or friends will perceive you?

Keep in mind the principle in that you never know who you might need in this world! You see it runs deep, and that's why you have to keep your emotions in check and maintain the course of configuration unless it's detrimental to your core. Don't (regress) to allowing your emotions to dictate your plans and actions, just as we discussed in the first book. Same principles apply here folks, just with a broader outlook beyond you. Just as from our prime example anybody who has worked for a significant amount of time should realize usually the people who have it easy at work are in good graces with not just their supervisor, but usually their supervisor's manager as well, and in most cases most of their coworkers. I say that in most cases because you never know how they obtained those good graces, but nevertheless good graces were obtained.

The main idea here is that it takes that type of stamina to configure minds well beyond your original host. Even if your host is being a good Shepard and spreading your good will as hoped, it's more than likely going to come a time in which you are going to be tested by those vicarious individuals as well. That's why you need to be ready at all times because it only takes that one lapse in configuration that could change anybody's perception of you at any time. For instance, what if the boss who you configured raves about you to their boss and for that action of your immediate superior, their boss sees you as a standout employee? Now let's say one day you get caught breaking the rules by your boss's manager. How do you think your boss's manager is going to look at the situation? Will he or she dismiss the prior configuration from your immediate supervisor as a lie? Will he or she question the judgement and evaluation of your supervisor? Will he or she rain down a storm of discipline on the department for your actions? How will your immediate supervisor feel after the one employee he or she has raved about let him or her down?

Think about that, and when you configure somebody to what you are about it must remain authentic! Point blank! This is why we are saying that laziness can't invade your mind when it comes to configuration. Remember the 24/7 factor! You never know where opportunity lies and you must remain steadfast on these principles at all times. Now with all this said (LOL), even though we said you never stop configuring someone who is vital to achieving a goal, remember the when factor, right! You got to know when to call it and seek a peaceful coexistence or abort configuration altogether if it's detrimental to your core. Let's dwell on the power of analyzing again and learn when to say when!

Chapter 9: Analyzing

Here we are again folks, utilizing the power of analyzing. Before we begin to detail how analyzing can aid or derail you from configuration, let us refresh our minds on what analyzing is. We previously defined analyzing as the input of fact and the suppression of emotion in order to find a resolution to a problem. This doesn't change here folks. Remember the principles don't change, only the situation to which they are applied. With that said, let's get to the meat and potatoes on how it works in regards to configuration. Keep in mind this should be something you should be applying to all aspects of your life in order to make sound decisions.

So, put it together, if you are analyzing someone in an effort to configure their mind to your goals, what exactly are you looking for? That's your homework for the day (LOL). However, since I'm such a good professor, I'll give you the answer. You should be looking for signs that your configuration is cementing itself in the person's brain, ineffective, slightly effective, too effective, or not worth it at all. Sounds familiar from the first book, just worded differently. Look, the way you analyze the host whom you are trying to infect means the world of importance. One mistake could derail the whole process if you misread your potential host. You can't ever reasonably assume that everybody is going to fall for your shit, as we have mentioned this earlier in this book. Therefore, it's crucial you analyze the person who you are trying to configure precisely in order to configure or not have any negative repercussion come back on you as well. This is just as crucial so remember that!

For example, there have been many bullies who picked on the wrong person, right? There have been many millionaires who are mistaken to be poor every day. There are many geniuses who were stereotyped as ignorant. There have been many people who got the shock of their life when they first fucked their spouse for good or for worse (LMAO). I can give you some stories on that shit, for good and worse, but that's another book. At any rate, I think you get the picture. Wise man once said, "You can't judge a book by its cover!" I love this quote as it emphasizes the core of what analyzing prevents and affirms at the same time!

Never ever assume that a person is what they are through prejudiced thoughts, also known as an opinionated mindset, which is a no, no, anyways! Read the definition again while you keep in mind that you will never ever exactly know a person, but at the very least you can reasonably assume some if not the majority of their character by analyzing their words coupled with their actions. This is on a continuous basis without ever coming to a solution of "I know this person completely." Never! So, with that said, you analyze your host accordingly and under the 24/7 factor, reconfigure, commence, or stop configuration altogether depending on the data you receive.

For example, let's say you are trying to woo a potential new lover who you encounter on a regular basis. Let's say it's a neighbor because of the close proximity. What would be your course of action to try to configure their mind to entertaining a possible relationship with you? This is when a good plan comes into play. Same principles here folks, same principles! Now whatever plan you set forth will be what it is as it pertains to your core, but it should at the very least have these basic guidelines. They should be getting the host's attention, start a dialogue, get to know the person based off analyzing (reasonable assumption), see if the person is even worth it to pursue, obtain a date, get laid, start a relationship, and more from there on. Again, plans will vary depending on the individual, but those should be some basic objectives of your plan.

The actions you deploy again will vary, but at the core of all those actions should be the method of achieving a relationship. Now here's what we are saying as it pertains to analyzing. Whatever words or actions you deploy, under the 24/7 factor, you should be analyzing each reply from your potential host of your words just as well as their actions in response to your actions! You need to analyze this in order to give you a window into what direction your host is possibly going. Are they on the fence, are they falling in line, are they repelling your advances, are they leery of you, or are they even worth it to pursue?

Wise man once said, "You can't trust smile and a pretty face!" That was for the women (LOL)! Wise man once told men "Can't trust a big butt and a smile!" So true folks, so true in both scenarios! So, if you are paying attention, you should see how all principles are coming together here even as we are focusing solely on the analyzing portion of our interwoven scheme. Everything is interwoven here folks, everything!

So, you are analyzing your host for configuration to a relationship. Thus, you should be collecting data on key components on the tell all signs of acceptance: body language, the host's own words, their actions, for better, or worse. You should look for these signs in efforts to gauge your potential host's temperature. Now obviously, if you get direct answers like "Yes, I'll go on a date with you," which are easy to decipher, that's fine, but it doesn't mean anything until your ultimate objective is reached. Before we even get further ahead, keep in mind before you even get to this point, those initial engagements of configuration should be geared towards is this person worth it!

Remember, analyzing has an underlying value of timing. Knowing when to say go or knowing when to say hell no. This is important because you don't want to waste time in any scenario. You definitely don't want to waste time in getting laid (LOL). On the other hand, you definitely don't want to waste time beating a dead horse. That time could be used on pursuing a more suitable candidate, right!

So, with that said, we also keep in line with the laws of never taking anything for face value. You have to be a journalist when it comes to getting at one's true motives. The first thing that anyone who is entering the field of journalism should be taught or have the basic understanding of is investigation. Nothing indifferent than what we have been stressing already, as per the scientific method. The only difference is rather than configuring your own mind and answering yourself essentially, you are questioning others about others in order to come up with some possible motives of your hosts.

For instance, a journalist should investigate multiple sources in order to accurately substantiate their reports on a particular subject matter. If they fail to do so, they can stand the risk of losing their reputation, losing their job, and even possibly being sued. You see, a reporter's reputation for delivering truthful information is very important when it comes to configuring the minds of his or her viewers. Their reporting helps shape the views of many and impacts could be felt across multiple dimensions of society such as politics, finances, healthcare, shopping, etc.

When you are analyzing your host to see if your shit is soaking in, you need to keep this in the back of your mind. Explained differently, but again folks, same principles. If you fail at configuring your host, the reputation you garnered will be lost and you too will fall victim in the same way as a shunned journalist. This is why it is important to evaluate throughout the process (analyzing) if you are making headway, need to change your approach, or abort altogether. Understand this, even if you do lose configuration, that doesn't mean that it's an end all fail of configuring that host. Depending on the severity of the mishap, there still may be a chance of recouping that host, or salvaging other relationships connected to that individual, and even maintaining a peaceful coexistence. However, it shapes up, you still have to be able to foresee this coming, preferably before catastrophic shit happens.

This is the whole purpose of analyzing, right, trying to do your best at not falling victim to a problematic plan. So again, you have to be a journalist and never take face value as an assured sign your configuration is working. Understand this next step for your purpose and your host as well. Anything that is deemed to be fact should always at a rate of 100% be able to withstand any investigation that comes its way. This is critical folks, and it still remains in the confines of our principles.

Remember we stated earlier that you need to display and have a proven track record aligned with your host's values as well, right! Same in reverse, you need to know that your host is in collusion with your values as well. Anybody can shake your hand, agree with you, have sex with you, etc., but are they truly down with your cause? You have to test that theory consistently! I do mean very consistently at best. Remember, you can't afford to wait until shit collapses. You want to be ahead of the curve. This is why so many people fail at configuring others, because they don't scrutinize the perceived facts right in front of them.

When someone says they love you, it needs to be tested in all the many aspects of what love entails. When an accountant says your taxes are all done, you need to double check to ensure no errors were made. When you go to a fast food joint, you need to check your food and ensure it is what you ordered and inspect it for quality. When you go to the auto mechanic, you need to investigate the mechanic's findings to see if the diagnosis is accurate and not a scam. When you hire a home contractor, you need to investigate if their findings are factual or a scam! Never take anything at face value!

Again, a fact should be able to stand up to an investigation. Once you gather your own facts and deploy tests against your host, your host's original actions or words should be able to hold up in court! By the way folks, just like a journalist, your own investigation should be the main component in determining the truth. You see, before you even go to that auto mechanic, you should have already committed yourself to diagnosing your car's problem via unbiased sources, such as a car manual, a friend, car supply stores, or even the internet. Then you should go to the mechanic now as an educated customer and cross reference that initial mechanic with at least three other mechanics' findings. If they all match up and are in line with your investigation, more than likely you have found the remedy for your car. The only thing left now is to get it repaired at the cheapest price or even do it yourself!

You see how that works folks? Is it easier to just accept the so-called professional? Is it more convenient just to get it done and not follow all the other steps of analyzing your car's problem? Sure, if you want to run the risk of getting fucked out of your money, go ahead! Get this folks, it's not just your money you will possibly lose, it's your reputation, and this is what will ultimately continue to fuck you. Think about it like this, if I know I can get over on you without repercussions, don't you think I'm going to do so? That same mechanic that you now have entrusted off face value is now fattening his or her pockets off your misery. Hell, I wouldn't be surprised if they start rigging your car to fail because you have configured their mind that you're gullible.

This happens in the world everyday folks; simply put there are predators and there is prey. What side are you on? Many people have been fucked because they thought they had a person configured to help them achieve their goals.

Moreover, a lot of people don't even find out they're getting fucked unless from a mishap by the predator or if they ever find out at all. This is why you need to carefully analyze your host. It is vital to configuration as so stated a million times. Put your host to the test. It is the only way to get an accurate read on where you stand within their mind. We said it before, it is an ongoing process that will cause for numerous tune ups along the way, but ultimately when done right, it should help your reach your goals.

So, let's discuss some methods of testing. Remember you're a journalist trying to find out if your host is accepting your configuration or not. You need only to start with yourself, as always in everything you do. What persuasions have you uploaded to your host's mind? What's the reason for this configuration, as we stated earlier? What signs are you looking for to gauge whether or not your configurations are working? How many parties are involved in this particular configuration? Because remember we said you are not only configuring the host but all who the host is encountering as well.

Now is when your interpersonal skills come in to play. How well can you open a person up and talk to their soul? We mentioned earlier in the book that it is key to reciprocate whatever good your host is doing for you. It doesn't exactly have to be match for match but you need to align yourself with their goals so long as it's not negatively impacting you. For instance, if a friend treats you for dinner you might want to treat them next time around. Another equivalent would be something like treating them to a drink at the bar, a movie, dinner at home, etc. The point is if your host is donating their resources to your cause whether it is money, time, shelter, etc., you need to reciprocate in such a manner. It's a must without exception!

This reciprocation process shouldn't be forced, however. It should come from you and more importantly your host as natural as breathing. If you come into a realm where you are bending over asshole backwards, your host is bending over asshole backwards, or the both of you are bending over asshole backwards to please each other, there's a problem. That means there's an air of untrustworthiness, poor configuration tactics, your ass is the one actually being configured, or you lost configuration altogether. All of which are less than ideal; nevertheless, they can be used for great diagnostic signs when trying to configure someone.

Understand this, if a person has to be forced to align themselves with your goal, then there is a high possibility that they aren't really down with you! You need to be able to see these tell all signs before you go asshole backwards trying to configure a dead horse. Think of it like this. When you purchase an album from an artist, they are not holding a gun to your head making you purchase it, right? You purchase it on the quality of music or whatever your reasons are. There is no force involved, and the artist has successfully configured your mind to purchase their music. They did so by putting in time crafting songs and making videos in an effort to please your ear buds! You then reciprocated by purchasing their music. It's a win, win situation. The entertainer delivered a song that moves your spirit, and you paid them for their efforts. This is not a lateral reciprocating tactic like dinner for dinner per se, but it is an example of reciprocating nonetheless.

We mentioned earlier how people derail configuration by trying to push their agenda on people too soon or too brute. Let it flow naturally with a smooth delivery of configuration tactics. You don't have to force it! Now as far as those tactics, the rules don't change: patience, strong interpersonal skills, emotionless tactics, facts only, scientific method, planning, and analyzing. This all sounds familiar, right? A lot of people fuck up configuration by forcing people to align with their cause. For example, you'll be surprised at how many people ruined the possibility of a good relationship from the door. Some people bend asshole backwards trying to woo their potential partners by lavish gifts, always paying for dates, having sex too soon, catering to the other's interests all the time, and more. Think about the configuration going on here.

Wise man once said, "I was this way when you met me," and that same wise old owl probably also said, "The way you got me is the way you keep me." Think about how many relationships have ended because of lack of sex like it was in the beginning, a partner not showering the other with gifts like they used to in the beginning, a partner dressing too sexy like they did when you met them but now it's inappropriate since you are in a relationship, a partner not spending anytime with the other like in the beginning, etc. I mean the list just goes on and on, but the key takeaway here is the flawed configuration that deployed from the start. If you read the first book prior to this one, you should already be well balanced within yourself with a solid understanding of you. You need that before configuring others, as we so have mentioned mucho already, because it is that mathematical process of your core times your host's core divided by commonality, which will derive an answer of this person's worth to your goals.

For example, your core should always be consistent of getting reciprocation from whoever you are dealing with no matter what. Thus, with that said when you treat a date to dinner the first time, you should expect them to pick up the tab the next time. Now, let's say you picked up the tab on the first date and now you're engaging in conversation and getting to know this potential host (analyzing). This is pretty typical, right, but this initial meeting is key in configuration. You need to ask questions as some people often do, but most really don't try and get down to someone's core. So, using our mathematical process we just explained, lay out your questionnaire. Now keeping in mind that you already have a solid core and foundation, gear your questions in efforts of compatibility not conformity! If you conform to your host how are you going to be able to compare and contrast? Moreover, you are likely getting your ass configured. These are not desirable conditions. Your questions need to be direct, indirect, serious, humorous, and then tested through your host's actions.

What I mean by direct and indirect is asking the same question but in different ways. What I mean by asking serious and humorous questions is inquire about what you want to know directly but essentially adding a joke or two to lighten the air. You'll be surprised at how many people get afraid and run from strong minded individuals. At the same time, this is good because it weeds out your potential threats to your goal. On the other hand, if at the end of this initial meeting you find your host has potential to aid you, then their ass can't go anywhere! Humor is a great tool in regulating the emotions in people's mind! It all goes under the umbrella of killing them with kindness. Same principles folks, deployed differently.

Last but not least, as self-explained, test your host's words by their own actions and your actions. This goes under the umbrella of not taking face value as fact. So, to put it into perspective per our example of the date, deploy these strategies. Let's say your core is to have a partner that has strong ambitions and are gainfully employed. Your direct line of questioning should be what do you do for a living. This is typical direct straight forward dialogue. Let's say your date's response is that they are a music artist. Ok, cool, you have an answer. Now you want to go indirect with the questioning. Keep in mind your host might already have replied ahead of the curve in your anticipation of gathering what you want to hear, but you still need to question them indirectly on the same line, same way somehow.

A wise man once said, "It is much harder to maintain a lie then it is the truth!" Asking questions directly and indirectly will give you a good gauge on your host's true depiction of themselves through their consistency. Remember it should be validated with time and action, but at least you can start to paint the picture through the host's words. With that said, a good indirect question would be where do you see yourself in 20 years if you are not in the music industry? You see, since part of your core is to have someone with ambition and gainful employment, you need to gauge how dedicated one is to their career, and do they have back up plans to keep the money coming? You see, if you just ask where you see yourself in 20 years, the obvious response is probably going to be still a music artist selling millions of albums, being rich and famous, etc.

However, when you throw that monkey wrench in the questioning on what you would do without music, you then start to touch on the inner workings of the host's mind (testing them)! If your host responds in a precise and organized manner, that's a good sign. Moreover, use that response to check their dedication level to their goals in life. I would want to expect that if a person can't make it as an artist per se, they should still want to be around music in some capacity, whether earning a living or chasing their dream while earning a living in a different industry.

So then, you want to lighten the mood because you were asking some serious questions, right. I might say something like, "Can I have your autograph? Even if your album flops, I will be your number one fan," or some shit like, "If you ever work in one of those restaurants that sing happy birthday to the customers, you'll kill it if the music biz don't work out!" (LOL) You know little things like that, but despite the humor, you are encouraging your host to reveal their true nature.

For instance, if your host replies, "Oh hell no, not me never" to working in a restaurant, that is giving you key insight on your host's true nature. It could mean that there is a certain limitation in which they are willing to earn a living. It could also mean that they place themselves in high regard, that they are dedicated to making it in the industry, that they are swayed by their emotions, etc.

121

Remember everything is cohesive. Thus, if one of the principles is impacted it will affect another part of the system. You have to remember to constantly tie it all together to get the full picture. This is why balancing the mood is so important because you get more bang for your buck, so to speak. In essence, you get the most optimal answer when balancing a serious and humorous approach to your questioning.

Now following the scientific method, it's time to put your host to the test on their words by their actions and how they gauge your actions. For instance, if someone tells me that music is their sole means of earning a living, I want to see how they are living. Analyze their housing situation, such as where they live, how they live, cost of their living, etc. Analyze their clothing, such as brands they wear, type of clothing, etc. Then you want to see what exactly they do as an artist. An industry such as music takes extreme dedication and talent. Thus, I would want to hear some materials, see how they market themselves, are they touring, how they make the money, etc. If a person comes to me and says they are an aspiring artist, then I would expect them to be on a strong grind trying to get discovered. With that said, a good answer for me coupled with the host's actions for validity would be the host telling me, "I earn a living as a studio singer, backup singer, song writer, producer, and I produce my own music." Again, those words coupled with the fact that you actually see them doing it helps validate who the truly are.

On the other hand, if someone comes up to me and says they are an aspiring artist with no true income coming in and then tells me, "I'm waiting for my audition on a TV show to blow up," I have reservations about their character. It's as simple as that folks, but you have to trust the process. When we say use these principles, it's not just a one stop shop line of questioning. Rather it's a continuous process under the 24/7 factor in order to come up with a rational decision. You keep up the process every question every time in order to gauge whether or not your configuration is working or not.

Now, as you are observing their actions per their own words, you must also pay close attention on how they are viewing you. For instance, let's say one of your questions was, "How do you feel about me hanging out with my friends a lot?" and your date's response was, "I don't mind that at all." Then let's say six months into the relationship that you are a couple and spend a lot of time with your friends, and your partner now is starting to become frustrated with it. Their actions are now conflicting with what they said initially. This should be a red flag for you as they observe your actions in which supposedly, they said they were ok with. This could possibly end the relationship from the partner's perspective and yours. Now for simplicity I said six months, but it could be one, two, three, eight, or even 10 years before the partner showed their true nature. Remember you're in it for a long haul configuring someone's mind. Thus, analyzing the host's words and actions is crucial just as well as being able to terminate configuration if it's no longer aligned with your goals.

You ever hear people say they are just with their spouse out of convenience? What type of life is that? People who say these types of things are willing to settle to a life of opportunity lost. They have given up on their goals. Their core and foundation have dissolved to worthlessness. You see these principles of humanology and how to configure other's mind forces you to keep your goal in sight and at the same time protects you from an oppressed mindset (regression). You see, at this point when your host's actions are starting to contradict their words, you need to figure out if that is crucial to your happiness. This is how our mathematical process of your core time host's core divided by commonality gives you the answer of their importance in your life. You see once you established that you and your host's core are aligned multiply them together. Think of the core in this instance as a vehicle driving on a road to goals. Then divide those core values by how many times you and your host will go in the same direction and opposite direction.

Here is where you can compare and contrast to determine what elements you would consider to be a peaceful coexistence, a cause for configuration termination, or a cause to configure. For instance, your core values as far as cuisine might be aligned but parenting techniques might differ. If your core of parenting ranks higher than food, then it wouldn't be wise to try and configure this person to have your child or even pursue a relationship. Vice versa if food is more important to you then you might want to pursue a relationship and find a peaceful coexistence on parenting. That decision is up to you but you need to be in it to win, be happy, and never miserable. This leads us to how not to enter the corridor of misery, and that's reevaluation.

Chapter 10: Reevaluation

So, as we said in the first book, reevaluation is a great tool to deploy in order to avoid regression. As a refresher, reevaluation helps you resist the temptations of beating a dead horse to rise or running into a dead end. The principle doesn't change, only the situation. The situation, as it pertains to the first book, was analyzing your own condition after a systematic approach to achieve a goal. That situation tweaks a little as now you are analyzing the condition from which your host and those aligned with him or her are in after your systematic approach to configure them all! Don't forget, however, that the core of the principle still remains intact. You also must simultaneously decide whether conditions are right for you and should you cease or resume configuration.

With that said, your reevaluation breakdown should be something along the lines of answering if this configuration is still crucial in order for me to achieve a goal. Do I still need all the people in the hub in order to reach my goal? Were there unforeseen circumstances, in which I didn't plan for, that has caused a shift in momentum of my configuration? Have I overachieved on my configuration? Is there a better way to achieve my goal without the host or hosts I'm trying to configure? Was my plan of configuration flawed? What changes are necessary in order to recapture or maintain configuration? Am I able to maintain configuration? Are there new people involved in the hub that need to be configured as well, etc.! It gets really comprehensive and tedious, but answering these questions is extremely necessary in order to get configuration right. You should always think of your configuration as a chain link that connects the primary host to all who are aligned with them, and as they say it only takes one loose link to disrupt the integrity of a chain.

Again, I repeat, ensure that you gauge at least the key individuals within your host's inner circle because you need to either suppress or enhance their feeling towards you in order to configure your primary host. For example, when you get into a relationship with a new person, who should you automatically have on your list for configuration, other than your primary new spouse? Who are the key players you think are in the inner circle? Well using the scientific method, you can make an educated guess (hypothesis) and say at the very essence of social norms more than likely some key people in the person's life might be their parents, siblings, kids, relatives, pet, job, best friend, hobbies, etc. Now I want you to play close attention here, as I said hobbies and job. Now someone who isn't a student of this science called humanology might not understand why these entities are important. To put it quite frankly and as we spoke on earlier, regardless of what you do on a day to day basis, you are going to have to interact with another human in one way or another. With that said, it is just as important to know what kind of culture exists around your partner's professional career and also what type of culture exists around their hobbies.

For example, ladies, what would you think of the man or woman who you became involved with in a platonic relationship when all of a sudden, he or she becomes the owner of a strip club? At the same time, men, how would you feel if your partner became dancer at a strip club? To some it may be acceptable, to some it may be deal breaker, and to some it may cause a bit of uneasiness. Whatever the scenario that is aligned with your specific core will vary, but the principle remains that these entities such as strip clubs need to be scrutinized for what they are worth and what benefits or negative traits they bring onto you.

This goes without saying to hobbies as well. If your spouse likes to go to dance clubs, you should analyze that and be able to conjure up what impacts that type of lifestyle would have on you. For instance, your thought process should include but not be limited to how does the social scene in a dance club impact my relationship? What undue influences exist in dance clubs? What specific types of cultural norms exist in the spouse's favorite music? Where is the location of the dance clubs? How often does my spouse engage in this hobby, etc.? These are all questions in which you need to have a clear picture of in order to make a sound judgement on whether or not to configure this person to a relationship.

Now before I get into my soap box with explanations of what I mean, I want you to catch the text that the spouse in the example all of a sudden became an owner of a strip club. Hence, they weren't a business owner when you met them. It is with fair warning to note again that configuration takes time and a whole lot of adaptability in order to maintain or even discontinue configuration. Humans often change over the course of time, some few, some often, some here and there, but the common core of all is that we all change. Health, living, and learning changes practices and habits. This is why it is so important to be able to adapt to change and still maintain your pursuit of happiness.

We just touched a bit on why a person's hobbies are important to analyze, right! Now tie it together with being a chameleon and having the ability to either blend in with your surroundings to fit in safely while you hunt (consider this maintain configuration) or being able to shadow yourself from harm and escape a predator's grasp (consider this breaking configuration)! So, let's say your spouse loves to dance and you practically accompanied them when they went out all the time. Now let's say you had a health crisis that caused you to be permanently paralyzed from the waist down and you can't boogie anymore. On the other hand, your partner still wants to shake his or her ass and continue going to the club while you lay idle. How would you handle this situation? Remember folks, the principles are in cohesion with each other. Thus, when I said health crisis, it should have already been under your unforeseen circumstances department analyzing if you lost your legs, would this person still want to dance with you (maintain relationship under your configuration) or break it off (rejecting your configuration and now an antagonist to your happiness)!

You see this is why a wise man captured the phrase, "Do you take thee in sickness or health, 'til death do you part," in marriage vows. It is anybody's guess to say how each individual would react to this scenario because everybody's core is different. Nevertheless, it is reasonable to obtain a strong inclination of how it may play out under the scientific method and humanology principles. For the sake of the example, let's say the couple remained together. What strategies would you deploy in both spouse's mind, the injured and the party animal, in order to maintain configuration? Again, this is whether knowing your core and foundation intertwines with configuring other individual's minds to your goal; in this instance it's a relationship. Both parties should have a clear assessment of what lies in front of them now and in the future, given the cards that they have been dealt (reflections). Then there will have to be mutual reciprocation between both parties in order for each individual to achieve his or her happiness.

So, your analysis should be somewhere in the ballpark along these lines. For one, if all other core components are still aligned with your partner, are you willing to adapt to allowing them to party their brains out without you? At the same time, are you willing to tag along with your partner in a less mobile state in order for them to still be happy, as well as yourself? Now what about the party animal? Are they willing to cut back on the partying in order to tend to the injured spouse's needs and adapt to becoming a caretaker? This can go in so many different ways to fully elaborate on in one book. However, the synopsis here is that under the principle of reevaluation, you have to be able to pick up the pieces of a shattered configuration attempt and keep on trucking to reach your goals. This is going to take adaptation without emotional discharge, planning, reflection, standing on your core and foundation, deploying the use of facts only, refraining from regression, *The Core of Humanology,* right! This is why reevaluating your configuration of someone periodically enhances your ability not to succumb to a trapped situation.

Although if it happens, the principles of humanology teach us to still strive for at least a peaceful coexistence if not a victory, but never defeat or surrender! You see, the trick is to get out of an undesirable situation before shit rolls downhill when configuration of a host or hosts fail. By all means you want to at the very least not be the cause of making the situation difficult for yourself. That would be a significant sign of you falling off your core and foundation, which is never acceptable for failure, only enhancement.

Think about the power of reevaluating the configuration of another human and what traps could be avoided. How about breaking up with someone before you marry them! How about breaking up with a deadbeat before you have kids with them! How about looking at the job your barber or hairstylist performed on your head every time before you walk away and notice a chunk of your hair missing! How about counting your change every time you exit your favorite corner store! Assess, assess, and more assessment, folks. I can't stress enough how important that is to configuration. Keep the rule of thumb in the back of your mind that people change for good and for worse. The best tools in your arsenal to combat those changes are adaptability and constant reevaluation.

Think of it like this, how many major store chains have you seen fold up in recent years? Some say it's because of another store chain that caused the demise of the store brand that defaulted. However, is that true? The answer to that is a resounding no! If you look at all the major store fronts that have gone out of business, you will realize they all have a common cause for their demise. Simply put, they failed to keep up with new trends in their respective industry (adaptability) and failed to adhere to what their customer base desired (reevaluation). Those two simple principles alone cause once prominent business entities to crumble to the ground.

You'll also find that even in the later stages of trying to reinvent the wheel, if the company tried at all, it was too late because the customer had now aligned themselves to another company (lost configuration). You see, they assumed their successful model of business would stand the test of time (stagnant), and they failed to keep their clientele interested through new ideas or even adhering to popular trends (maintaining configuration). On that same note, since they didn't perform critical reevaluation, they missed ominous signs of death to the company, like brands they carry losing popularity, the boom of e-commerce, keeping track of customers leaving for competitors, developing strategies to steal customers from competitors, etc.

The same way a company could go from earning millions to bankruptcy in a glance is the same way you can go from achieving a goal and back to square one in an instance. Evaluation is no good unless you utilize the data that's been presented to you in a multitude of ways. Now what we just discussed were things a business should look out for when it comes to gathering critical data needed to draw upon a scientific resolution to a problem or confirm that a problem exists. The signs to look for with humans are simple: emotions, words, and actions. These signs, whether coupled with each other or disbursed independently, should give you a good sense of how your configuration is going. This is done with objectivity. Now remember, just because you are in the market of configuring doesn't mean you are the only one with that power! This is why we stressed in the first book that keeping your emotions in check is critical, not only for making sound decisions but also it becomes part of your antivirus software that helps thwart configuration of your mind.

The same goes for your actions and how we told you never to bend over asshole backwards. Again, this aids your antivirus system with repelling any attempt of configuration, especially as we told you never spill your whole life story as soon as you meet someone. Knowledge is power folks, and just as you are trying to use this information to configure your host's mind, they are trying to counteract you with information you have given!

Now again, words, actions, and emotions are excellent indicators to assess how well your configuration is going. Keep in mind that as we say indicator, this doesn't mean a one-time occurrence. This means a consistent display of a train of thought through the channels of communication, hence words, actions, and emotions. Understand this, as we alluded to earlier in the book, patience is of sheer necessity when configuring!

At this point in the discussion you will see once again why, but yet again everything is intertwined anyways. We stated how one can either destroy or set the foundation for configuring someone's mind in an instant. For example, have you ever met a couple, and either one or the other or both said they couldn't stand the other for one reason or the other and now behold they have been together for years raising a family? Have you ever heard someone say they don't like a particular food, but now they love it? Have you ever heard someone say they were going to quit their job in the first week of employment and are still there years later, happy or not? The common denominator here folks is rather simple. It took patience for each scenario to come to fruition, along with all the other principles of humanology we have discussed.

Just because your initial advances on someone's mind doesn't register at that particular point and time, it is still a step in the right direction. Reason being through the principles of *The Core of Humanology*, you are supposed to learn from your mistake and press on, right! Take the example of the person who didn't like a particular food and now loves it. Let's say that food was bananas. Now a person who hasn't configured their mind might just say to hell with bananas! I'm staying away, easy as that! Now you may say, well what's wrong with that no harm, no foul, no worries. True, until you think of it through the context of your health! You see, potassium plays a vital role in your body's ecosystem, and bananas are loaded with it. It's healthy for you. That's what I'm getting at. Hence, there's nothing wrong with not liking to eat them per se, but to knowingly deprive your body of this vital substance is a problem. A person with a configured mind as per the first book is going to address the situation as so.

First, I need to really see if bananas aren't my thing because I would like to get the benefits of them some way somehow. You are going to (reflect) in the mirror and say, "Why don't I like bananas? Is it the texture? Is it the taste? Does it feel like a dick in my mouth or what?" Come to conclusion from your core and foundation and set forth a strategy to configure your mind to getting the benefits from bananas that you are missing out on. So, if it's the texture, try it in a different style like fried, chips, or as a drink. If it's because it feels like a dick in your mouth, cut it up in small pieces (LOL). If at last all else fails and you just can't come to grips with the taste, you can always supplement your diet with a vitamin suitable to your taste (peaceful coexistence). You see, through the process of trying to configure your mind to accept bananas, you came to the crossroads of realizing your configuration wasn't working. Therefore, you came to the peaceful coexistence of even though I can't configure you banana, I'm still getting what I need from you through other channels. Moreover, I'm getting it through channels directly tied to you! Hence, some vitamins will have extract from bananas in them.

This holds true, just as we explained to you, that you are not only configuring the mind of another person but also all those who that person is connected with. So, as you are pursuing configuration on potential allies to your goals, patiently pay attention to detail. The idea is to use the scientific method to formulate a strong scenario on which direction your configuration is headed. You must be able to break down all the data of words spoken, actions taken, and emotions deployed by your potential host in order to draw on a strong possibility.

Before we continue, I want you to keep in mind your (objectivity) here because it is the main reason why I refrain from saying conclusion; instead I'm saying possibility. Again, as we said before, never ever come to the conclusion that you know someone like a book. You will never ever truly know someone unless you have their mind. What we are doing as configuration is merely creating a rental space if you will in the host's mind, but you will never actually truly own it! With that said, you will set your configuration up for failure assuming all is won and leave yourself vulnerable to attack from that same host as well.

Take this for example, say you meet someone, and you put in a plan of configuration to get them to be your new spouse. You wine and dine them. Your host seems to be into you. You have sex with your host, and at last the process is complete. You have a new partner. That's how it goes, right. Here's the thing! How you know that the partner actually wants a relationship? True, they could have said during dating all the right words, displayed consistent demeanor, and correct emotions, but how do you know they are sincere? Don't take my word for it. Think about all those folks who went through the exact same process only to find out that their partner either had a spouse already, was using them for what they needed at the time and bounced once mission accomplished, or did a complete 360 from what you knew of them when you were dating. You can reach out and literally touch millions of people with this story, and they all have the same common flaw of, "I though he or she loved me!" You can't subject yourself to such treachery and therefore you must always maintain a mindset of getting to know your host rather than thinking you already know them.

Understand this, in most scenarios, a person, through emotion, word, and action, will undoubtedly show you their true colors. You need only to wait, analyze, experiment, and draw a conclusion upon your observation. It's as simple as that for most individuals, but for those who are a little more cunning, it may take more time and possibly advanced techniques to get to their true nature. Whatever the case, their true nature will come forth. Humans are creatures of habit, and so as their mind goes, all subsequent theories on their depiction of reality shall follow from that set of rules. This is why you must let configuration happen organically.

You can never force configuration, only persuade it to happen. This is why people fall victim to reverse configuration because they try to force configuration to happen and end up losing objectivity. They become blind to the (facts) sitting right there in front of them. Wise man once said, "The truth will always come to the light." I love this quote, not for the literal version of its meaning, but the subliminal side of it. That subliminal meaning is that you must also accept not knowing the truth as the truth. You shouldn't ever assume you know what a person has, what they are capable of, their likes, their dislikes, etc. You'll be surprised at how many people don't take the time to pursue enlightenment on these topics of their host because they assume that they already know.

How do you know if you become critically ill your partner won't leave your ass? How do you know your kids aren't doing drugs? Are you around your kids 24/7 to know? Have you been critically ill yet to know if your spouse would stay by your side? This is why you have to get to a strong possibility that is either more than likely (fact), or the truth of the matter is that you just don't know. This is how you can ask do I marry this person or not right now. This is how you can ask do I trust my kids or should inspect and test them randomly. This is how you don't fall victim to other's configuration.

You see, people are so afraid of failure usually disguised in the phrase, "I don't want to start all over again," that they actually choose to avoid the truth or pursing the unknown altogether. Wise man once said, "Sometimes when you win you actually lose, and sometimes when you lose you actually win and sometimes when you win or lose you actually tie (peaceful coexistence)." Think of it like this: you might have kids that respect you but is it worth the expense of them becoming junkies? You may have a husband or wife, but is it worth them leaving you when you are critically ill? Yes, you have obtained goals of well-mannered kids and getting married, but that win is a lost in the long run. On the other hand, if you stay on your kids' asses about drug usage and test your spouse on how much they care for you from time to time, you win. Sure, you may lose some like points from your kids and place some burden on your spouse, but that minor love lost is a win. Finally, if you kids become outraged and refuse to adhere to your policies, kick their ass out of your house. At the same time, if your spouse becomes annoyed by taking care of you during minor episodes of illness, then you might want to kick their ass out the house as well.

There are no winners or losers here, but you reach your goal of a peaceful coexistence. You see leaving your spouse leaves the way for someone who might be willing to stay by your side at critical times, and kicking the kids out alleviates the stress of people doing drugs under your roof or disobeying your orders. We are going to continue this discussion of knowing when to stop or continuing configuration of someone's mind in the next chapter along with advanced techniques for those who are out to configure as well.

The last point we want to make here in this chapter is that to understand what we are going to explain in (facts only) is that you must come to grips with the hard truth and acknowledge the unknown. It would suck to be with someone for many years only to be dropped like a hot potato because you become ill or having to bury your kids because they died from drug abuse. There is a thin margin between victory and defeat, and most are determined by what people do with the facts that are right in front of their eyes. Configuration is not a game folks, whether it's your mind or someone else's. This is to keep you employed, keep you with shelter, food, water, clothing, friends, determine enemies, make good decisions, not get taken advantage of, be a better parent, etc. This is your one-way ticket through life, and you have only one shot to live it up! Let's dwell on the facts!

Chapter 11: Facts Only

You know there's nothing like a good, old, and downright fact. It is the undisputed characteristic in a discussion. It is without judge, jury, opinion, prejudice, or emotion. It simply is what it is! You see what a fact does for you is help you come to a reasonable conclusion without the antagonist just mentioned above. As we mentioned in the first book, making decisions off a factually based substance shields you from falling victim to emotions and other viruses just mentioned. You see, even though a person may have all the facts in front of them, their emotions could still sway them to engage in risky behavior.

One prime example that sums up this notion is sex. Think about how many people fall victim to their emotions when they get a little horny (LOL). They end up meeting somebody and sleep with them right away to cure that itch. On the other hand, they don't really know the person from a can of paint! They don't know the full extent of their personality, lifestyle, or health. This happens everyday folks, to a neighbor near you, but what risks does this behavior carry? You already have the fact that you truly don't know this person. Is this night of passion worth your health? I mean, you don't even know if you're going to get satisfied! I'm sure you can find plenty of people out there who wish they could have refrained from some encounters.

Wise man once said, "Everything that shines ain't gold!" I love this quote because it stresses the importance of analyzing facts as a part rather than the whole. For instance, as the quote explains, just because you see a well-dressed person walking down the street, that doesn't mean they have an affluent job. Just because you see a provocatively dressed woman on the street doesn't mean she's a prostitute, and just because you see a man begging for money on the street doesn't mean they are homeless. You see, the average perception that goes along with these scenarios are social prejudices conjured up by the masses, but confirmation of such titles for these individuals can only be ascertained by fact. You see, this notion expands a little bit on what we told you about the principle of facts only in the first book because when configuring the minds of others, you must stay vigilant while on the lookout for frauds.

You see, the first book was about you getting your mind configured, and as a wise man once said, "I know I'm not going to lie on myself!" On the other hand, however, someone out there is willing and able to tell you a bold-faced lie in order to advance their agenda. Remember, just as you are out there configuring folks, so are others. Don't get caught up in a lie becoming the truth. The only thing undisputed in a discussion of validity is a fact. You must use it wisely when trying to configure someone's mind in order to develop the right strategies of maintaining configuration, configuring, or deploying a peaceful coexistence.

For instance, when a group of people are in a discussion about who's the greatest athlete in a particular sport, you can bet your ass there's going to be an abundance of pennies on the floor (for you slow folks that means a lot of people giving their two cents on who's the best ever)! Each person is going to have their own assessment. Some that are aligned with each other of course, but you will truly have a wide range of people lobbying for their candidate as the best. You see, this is the discussion part of this particular instance of trying to configure folks to your position, right! Accordingly, within this discussion you are going to discuss statistics, all-star appearances, championships, MVP's, etc. Now you will hear numerous opinions. However, the undisputed (facts) here will be the statistics themselves! You see, no matter how much the group debates, they will undoubtedly never come to a consensus of who's the best. What they will come to though is who has the most MVP awards, all-star appearances, points, championships, etc. You see, they can debate the most clutch, fastest player, toughest player, etc., but the stats are actual (facts)!

Does this mean you can truly say that one player was better than another or the best ever? You see, you can say that this player is the best scorer ever by statistics, but can you say they are the best scorer ever besides stats? If you said yes, then you lack objectivity when it comes to configuring the minds of others. If you said no, then you are deploying the principle of objectivity and rightfully so refraining from essentially saying you know someone or something when you'll truly never know them both. Follow me folks, think of it like this. How many species have been deemed extinct only to be found thriving and alive? How many times has the theory on space changed? How many times have people wrongfully been incarcerated, then exonerated due to new evidence? And to our sports example, how many times in sports we have said there will never be another, and yet seemingly someone comes out of nowhere and surpasses them?!

The theme here is you are what a wise man once said, "You can't call it 'til you see it!" When talking facts that quote and this wise man suggestion of "seeing is believing" is the only way of deeming something absolute and true. Meaning, unless your eyes can stretch all corners of the globe, every nook, crevice, ocean, forest, street, alleyway, home, apartment, sewer, etc., how can you in absolute certainty deem a species extinct? If you never have seen a player play before television was invented, if you've never seen a player play to full capacity due to injury, if you've never seen amateurs play on a playground, if you have never seen players play before your time, if you never have seen players play after your time, and I do mean all of them, how do you determine the best you ever saw? I'm sure that there is an amateur out there right now that would whip a professional's ass any time of day.

You see, this is why you have to departmentalize your facts because they don't always paint the whole picture. In fact, they rarely ever will. What they will do, however, is aid you in painting the picture so that you can make a decision on where you stand in your attempt to configure, maintain configuration, or achieve a peaceful coexistence. You see, falling victim to the narrative of knowing is to regress off deploying the principle of using facts only because you don't know! You will never truly know but what you will know are the facts! Take for instance, every person begging for money on the street doesn't mean they are homeless. Rather could they be configuring folks to think they are to get some easy cash. I'll give you a prime example.

I drive pass a group of homeless folks every day. Now from the onset, they appeared homeless wearing torn clothing and the whole appearance of tragedy. Then I started to notice what was constant was their tattered clothing, but the men's facial hair was well groomed, and the women actually seemed to have had their hair dyed. Interesting right, how the fuck a homeless person can afford a haircut and perm over food! I said to myself perhaps it's a fluke, but I'll monitor the situation closely. That consistency of well grooming continued, and on top of that, I then noticed one particular so-called homeless person wearing an expensive leg brace. Now I'm totally like, hold the fuck up here, I got insurance and can't get that type of equipment, how does a homeless person afford such!

If you are analyzing accordingly, as you should be, your antennas are pointed sky high at this point right! So, I'm lamenting in my mind at this point that either these folks are some very lucky homeless people coming up on some good fortune from others, or they are a sham. I want you to understand that the reason why I bring this story up is, for one, it's true. Second, it shows you how you can be configured by others, and three, I'm actually a kindred spirit and don't mind helping my fellow man. However, just as I'm not only the author of this book, I'm also a client, and people must prove to me they are who they are before I deemed them fact!

So, with the facts that I gathered, I was already extremely apprehensive at this point about gifting these folks some cash. Now even as I say I was apprehensive, keep in mind I never said for fact I knew they were homeless. I'm just saying shit wasn't adding up! Finally, almost a year has gone by at this time, and while I was shopping in a grocery, guess who I see. Hell yeah, you said it, the homeless folks in line ahead of me in the grocery store. Their total bill came up to about $150. Some of their groceries included raw meats and other shit that either needed refrigeration or cooking. Did I also fail to mention they were well dressed and well groomed? So, I had to ask myself again, what homeless person you know buys shit that needs to be refrigerated and cooked if they don't have the means to do so? Long story short, that sealed it for me not to say they weren't actually homeless, but to say they weren't getting my damn money! Keep in mind, that even if I hadn't seen them in the store, they still weren't getting my money anyway because the facts in front of me couldn't be ignored. Again, I couldn't use those facts to be absolute in my thought whether they were homeless or not, but I can use the facts to safeguard the integrity of the usage of my hard-earned money.

This, ladies and gentlemen, is how you use facts to formulate a plan of action to configure someone. At the same time, keep yourself from falling victim to someone's configuration. Facts aren't to be used as the basis of a plan. Rather, they should be used as part of the plan. As I alluded to earlier, if you have your own mind configured properly, then you shouldn't be blind to the facts at this point. It is crucial that you are not because you will truly fail at configuring the minds of others. If you lie to yourself and run from the truth, you are that much more susceptible to accepting the lie of others essentially falling victim to their configuration of you.

I want you to keep in mind that when I say victim, I don't mean in a negative way all the time. It actually can be an influence of negativity, positivity, or both. What we are saying here is that it is not a good idea to be under the influence of others without your consent or knowledge. How will you be able to gauge what's coming your way if you are incoherent? You see, if your mind is configured right, you are more likely to see a liar for what they truly are and treat them accordingly per your core and foundation. This is another reason why compartmentalizing facts is important because, as we have said all along, you stand to learn something from everybody. Thus, with that said, this is why we said when configuring you don't use facts as a basis of a plan but as a part thereof.

For instance, getting back to our example earlier about the wise man quote "Everything that shines ain't gold," let's say you ran into a nice-looking person and you pursued a relationship with them. Let's say your core at this point is to find a good person that has good sex, job, and their own home. Then, let's say you found that the person hits on one out of three core components you are looking for. Let's say the one component they hit on was sex but struck out on job and home. What do you do? This question lays heavy on your foundation, but at the very least what should not happen is you falling prey to their configuration of looking for a place to stay and free rent! Think about the facts in front of you! Now there can be millions of scenarios of why the person isn't working or doesn't have a place of their own, but that shouldn't deter you from the fact that their present situation is what it is. Now you can fuck them every which way you like and even enter a relationship with them, but you can't ignore the fact that the person isn't fully what you want. You would be surprised at how most people would turn a blind eye to the facts and allow this person to become a resident in their home because of good sex.

This happens all the time folks, and when things go sour, they are the same folks you see on talk shows hollering how you can do this to me when I did everything for you! Well, whose fault was that? The facts were in front of you, and you chose to ignore and fall prey. You see, at the very least it should be in your mind through the lens of (objectivity) that this person could be a fraud, and the reason they give for the situation they are in may be a lie. Time and the scientific method will help give you insight or a direct answer to why they are what they are, but the precursor to that entire fact finding is the validity in your face that they are currently without employment and a home. It can't be overlooked while you conduct your experiments looking for answers because this is your safety net. That's the difference of letting someone live off you and finding out it was a bad decision after finding them out than studying them from afar, not making that huge mistake, and pleasing at least one of your core values all in one shot.

This is how you should be utilizing facts to negate your emotions while advancing your agenda. So, as we said you are not only configuring the mind of your hosts but to all who they associate with as well, right. Accordingly, just as we explained earlier with the extinct animal example, if you can't physically see it, you can't claim such a fact to be valid. If it is crucial to your core and foundation, then you merely go on your own crusade to either confirm or deny claims. This doesn't mean that at the end of your journey you can hold the finding to be absolute in truth. At the very least you can formulate from your own point of view and not be victim to someone else's influence. This brings yourself closer to reality of the matter.

This is in the same light of configuring others and not allowing them to configure you. You have to understand that people have so many widespread agendas nowadays that it is difficult to say what they actually really want of you. This where people go numb to the facts because they are out here chasing answers that they may or may not get. I say more than likely not because you are not in another person's mind to know the absolute truth of their thoughts. With that said, why waste time chasing a ghost when you can grab actual substance!

One thing about facts is they will always lead you, if not to the truth, damn close to it. This is why it is important to refrain from judgement because if you are wrong when declaring something as a fact, you are going to have to somehow finagle your way back to configuration. It must be done folks. This is also where you can see why compartmentalizing facts is important, because even if you can't gain access to someone's mind via one channel, another lane may be open to use for configuration. For example, what is the first thing you should do when a friend approaches you and says another person had some unsavory words to say about you? You would first be surprised to know most people would automatically assume this to be fact. At the same time, you will also be shocked on how many people would use this information as judge and jury on the individual presumed to have said something unsavory. These are the minds of individuals who have yet to configure the own minds correctly.

The appropriate action is to objectively view the information being conveyed to you as suspect until proven fact, if it can be proved! This is of course being done by using the scientific method, right. You are trying to find out if your friend is actually telling the truth, is your friend lying, what motive does your friend have for telling you this, is the information true, if the information isn't true, why your friend lied, if it is true why is this person speaking ill of you, what is the other person's motive, and much more! These questions have to be answered in order to formulate plans and configure folks to your goals. Think for a second, how do you know your friend isn't trying to ruin your relationship with the other person for whatever motive? How do you know the other person isn't trying to do the same? I mean literally folks, the reasons could be endless, but the main idea here is getting to the facts and concluding with substance that can be deemed the truth through action and word.

Then let's say you find out that one or the other person has some malicious intent to destroy you in some way. This doesn't mean you immediately discontinue configuration of either person. It just means you take the facts as they stack up, analyze the situation to reassess the situation, forge new plans, and configure on. This is all in accordance that the nature of the crime isn't extremely detrimental to your core and foundation, of course. You plow forward and continue to hammer away if you deem that person vital to your success.

Keep in mind, everything here is intertwined, yes! And as we said earlier, you never let your right hand know what your left is doing! While you are conducting your experiments and drawing conclusions, it should all be done with neutrality and discretion. This mean you don't run up to the person who assumingly talked shit about you and say, "Hey my friend told me you were talking shit about me!" Let the truth come to you by fact not aggression. Hence, that's an emotion right!

Keep in mind you don't know who's telling you the truth, and you don't want to make a mistake and close the door on the wrong person. The only action you should take is conducting a discreet investigation, and nothing more. Think about it like this, how many younger folks you know got them a sugar momma or daddy? I mean, you see it all the time with these celebrities, right! Think for a second of who's configuring who for what and why they are doing so. This is about the only time you're going to hear me say this ever, but you don't have to have your mind configured to figure this shit out. It is obvious the older party involved is usually looking to stay young and vibrant, have sex with someone more appealing, or just have a trophy! There can be a multitude of reasons, but that's the usual. The younger person is more than likely looking for stability, money, and even acclaim. Again, there can be any amount of reasons to do so, but these just are a few. Now as you analyze it in totality, they are both configuring each other.

Here's the thing, as you age, naturally shit falls apart, right. It is what it is. Thus, what would a young person want with an older person in decline? I'm not saying that there aren't folks out there into that shit, to each his own, but on the norm it doesn't happen. This is how even though a young person may not be attracted to a particular older person in general, they can be attracted to that cash! Vice versa, this is how an older person who couldn't normally under even circumstances is able to attract a much younger person, configure them through the avenue of legal tender. Keep in mind when I say even circumstances, I mean the younger person may not be able to be persuaded if they are already are financially secure. Moreover, the older person wouldn't be able to persuade the younger person if they were broke!

The point here folks, is what a wise man once said, "When one door closes, another one opens!" This is how mortal enemies can become friends after years of war by accessing one door both have interests in. It is just that simple in theory, but make no mistake about it, it is difficult yet achievable. You just have to keep your facts in front of you and never wavier with your configuration to make your life better. Take this for instance, say I have a friend who through fact, I know was trying to secretly woo my wife. Let's say the configuration I placed in this person's mind was to get me free tickets to whatever. The question then becomes is this behavior detrimental to my core in which I should cease configuration and seek a peaceful coexistence, or should I keep the facts in front of me under discretion and continue to get my free tickets? You see, I wouldn't dare leave my wife alone with the asshole but I would most definitely play dumb and keep my tickets coming. Now would I consider this person a true friend, "HELL no," but would I keep that notion in their mind, "Yes!" You see, as long as he hasn't touched my wife, there's no harm nor foul. Why stop a good thing if it isn't detrimental? You just know how to treat this particular person accordingly and advance your agenda at the same time. It's a sweet science.

Facts will keep you in check with your emotions and balance with your plans. People are going to try and influence you in so many ways with lies being the main weapon of deployment. You have to be able to see through the clutter and get to their objectives. It may seem a bit overwhelming at first glance to try and configure the masses at once, but if you treat each case as an episode, you are going to find that the facts from other sources will soon prove to be the gel that comes together as a picture. You need only to run continuous analyzation under the 24/7 factor, which you should be doing anyways, and put the puzzle together. It is much harder to maintain a lie than the truth. It will come out eventually! You need only to thread the facts together and forge an educated solution to an antagonist to your goal.

Just as we used the example earlier of how your friend told you that somebody was talking of you in an ill manner, the facts may not actually come from those two parties. It can come from an acquaintance of yours, a friend of your friend, a friend of the shit talker, a friend of a friend of your friend, etc. It will come. And even if it doesn't come to fruition in a clear perspective, you still have the door open for going down another avenue of configuration. Have you ever had a friend that gave you some information that was credible but it was needed like 10 years ago? This is why you keep plugging away folks. You have to understand that even though others' bond may be tight at the moment, they can fracture in an instance. This is why we say that you are not only configuring the mind of your host but all of those they cohort with. This is intertwined as always, of course, with keeping your facts under neutrality and discretion because you never know which ally will pull through.

This is how you use facts to pull it all together and keep it open at the same damn time. You will have to keep training yourself to analyze and scrutinize almost everything your hosts do, but once you get the hang of it, it becomes second nature. Wise man once said, "It ain't easy, but somebody's got to do it!" So, it might as well be you. In fact, only you of configured mind can do it. We much rather it be you than somebody else!

Let's surmise this book as so, you have to deal with all walks of life, such as religion, creed, ethnicity, gender, orientation, personality, greedy, shy, lonely, haters, lovers, funny, evil, mentally challenged, and a whole host of new creatures to come. That's just the facts folks, and as we suggested earlier, only the fittest can survive. Take this last tidbit on for size, and I swear we are going to stop talking (LOL). There are so many people that try to run from particular elements in society, thinking that it's the remedy for serenity. Don't get me wrong; in a good amount of cases it probably works but let's be honest, in order to dictate that type of preference, you usually need mucho dinero! And even still you still have to deal with people vicariously. The average Joe usually has to play the cards they are dealt with and hopefully ascend to their aspirations from there.

Wise man once said, "You can run but you can't hide!" If you don't believe me just take a look at your local news sometimes and then ask yourself these questions. When has the suburbs ever had this much of a drug epidemic? Why is suicide across the board at an all-time high? Why must you watch your back when you go to the movies now? Why do you have to be on the lookout just walking down the street in any neighborhood now? The proof is in the pudding folks, in that the world has shrunk when it comes to the diffusion of ideology. With that said folks, the two key components from that are you can't run from it any longer, nor can you ignore it. You can't ascertain shit from a person nowadays based off looks, religion, color, and so forth. You really got to do your homework to get to know somebody. This is crucial to know because you have to know how to configure these types of folks. At the same time, you must be well diverse yourself to even begin to know how to crack somebody's mind, right!

Folks, use these principles to get ahead and stay ahead. The facts will never leave you astray. Objectivity will never leave you blind. Analyzing will never lead you to a dead end. Your core and foundation will never have you lost. Making plans will never leave you empty handed. Reflecting will never make you regress, and lack of emotions can actually cause you joy! Snack on that shit 'til next time, folks. Please remember to follow us on Twitter, Facebook, and YouTube for daily inspiration under BloomandCloudSolutions™. Please feel free to share any comments or perspectives with us as we are always eager to hear from you, my friends. Much success to you all and never give up on your ambitions!